THE ISLAND PRINCESS

JOHN FLETCHER

THIS EDITION PREPARED FOR THE
ROYAL SHAKESPEARE COMPANY

NICK HERN BOOKS

LONDON

www.nickhernbooks.co.uk

OTHER TITLES IN THIS SERIES

William Shakespeare
EDWARD III

Jonson, Marston and Chapman
EASTWARD HO!

John Marston
THE MALCONTENT

Philip Massinger
THE ROMAN ACTOR

This edition of *The Island Princess*
first published in Great Britain in 2002
as a paperback original by
Nick Hern Books Limited
14 Larden Road, London W3 7ST
in association with the
Royal Shakespeare Company

Cover design by RSC Graphics Department
Typeset by Country Setting, Kingsdown, Kent CT14 8ES
Printed by Biddles of Guildford

A CIP catalogue record for this book is available from
the British Library

ISBN 1 85459 695 0

THE ROYAL SHAKESPEARE COMPANY

The Royal Shakespeare Company is one of the world's best-known theatre ensembles.

The Company is widely regarded as one of the most important interpreters of Shakespeare and other dramatists. Today the RSC is at the leading edge of classical theatre, with an international reputation for artistic excellence, accessibility and high quality live performance.

Our mission at the Royal Shakespeare Company is to create outstanding theatre relevant to our times through the work of Shakespeare, other Renaissance dramatists, international and contemporary writers. Every year the Company plays to a million theatregoers at 2,000 performances, including over 50 weeks of UK and international touring.

We want to give as many people as possible, from all walks of life, a richer and fuller understanding and enjoyment of language and theatre. Through education and outreach programmes we continually strive to engage people with the experience of live performance.

The RSC's touchstone is the work of William Shakespeare. We are committed to presenting the widest range of Shakespeare's plays and demonstrating through performance the international and enduring appeal of his plays. We also want to inspire contemporary writers with the ambition of the Renaissance stage, presenting new plays alongside classical theatre.

The Company's roots in Stratford-upon-Avon stretch back to the nineteenth century. However, since the 1960s the RSC's work in Stratford has been complemented by a regular presence in London. But Stratford and London are only part of the story. Over 25 years of residency in the city of Newcastle upon Tyne have forged a profound link between RSC artists and audiences in the north east of England. Many of our productions also visit major regional theatres around Britain. And our annual regional tour sets up its own travelling auditorium in community centres, sport halls and schools in towns throughout the UK without access to professional theatre.

While the UK is the home of the Company, our audiences are global. The company regularly plays to enthusiastic theatregoers in other parts of Europe, across the United States, the Americas, Asia and Australasia. The RSC is proud of its relationships with partnering organisations in other countries, particularly in America.

Despite continual change, the RSC today is still at heart an ensemble Company. The continuation of this great tradition informs the work of all members of the Company. Directors, actors, dramatists and theatre practitioners all collaborate in the creation of the RSC's distinctive and unmistakable approach to theatre.

THE ROYAL SHAKESPEARE COMPANY

A PARTNERSHIP WITH THE RSC

The RSC is immensely grateful for the valuable support of its corporate sponsors and individual and charitable donors. Between them these groups provide up to £6m a year for the RSC and support a range of initiatives such as actor training, education workshops and access to our performances for all members of society.

The RSC is renowned throughout the world as one of the finest arts brands. A corporate partnership offers unique and creative opportunities, both nationally and internationally, and benefits from our long and distinguished record of maintaining and developing relationships. Reaching over one million theatregoers a year, our Corporate Partnership programme progresses from Corporate Membership to Business Partnership to Season Sponsor to Title Sponsor, and offers the following benefits: extensive crediting and association; prestigious corporate hospitality; marketing and promotional initiatives; corporate citizenship and business networking opportunities. Our commitment to education, new writing and access provides a diverse portfolio of projects which offer new and exciting ways to develop partnerships which are non-traditional and mutually beneficial.

As an individual you may wish to support the work of the RSC through membership of the RSC Patrons. For as little as £21 per month you can join a cast drawn from our audience and the worlds of theatre, film, politics and business. Alternatively, the gift of a legacy to the RSC would enable the company to maintain and increase new artistic and educational work with children and adults through the Acting and Education Funds.

For information about corporate partnership with the RSC, please contact Victoria Okotie, Head of Corporate Partnerships,
Barbican Theatre, London EC2Y 8BQ.
Tel: **020 7382 7132**.
e-mail: **victoria.okotie@rsc.org.uk**

For information about individual relationships with the RSC, please contact Graeme Williamson, Development Manager,
Royal Shakespeare Theatre, Waterside, Stratford-upon-Avon CV37 6BB.
Tel: **01789 412661**.
e-mail: **graemew@rsc.org.uk**

For information about RSC Patrons, please contact Julia Read, Individual Giving Manager,
Royal Shakespeare Theatre, Waterside, Stratford-upon-Avon CV37 6BB.
Tel: **01789 412661**.
e-mail: **julia.read@rsc.org.uk**

You can visit our web site at
www.rsc.org.uk/development

RSC EDUCATION

The objective of the RSC Education Department is to enable as many people as possible, from all walks of life, to have easy access to the great works of Shakespeare, the Renaissance and the theatre.

To do this, we are building a team which supports the productions that the Company presents onstage for the general public, special interest groups and for education establishments of all kinds.

We are also planning to develop our contribution as a significant learning resource in the fields of Shakespeare, the Renaissance, classical and modern theatre, theatre arts and the RSC. This resource is made available in many different ways, including workshops, teachers' programmes, summer courses, a menu of activities offered to group members of the audience, pre- and post-show events as part of the Events programme, open days, tours of the theatre, community activities and youth programmes. The RSC Collections, moved into a new home, will be used to create new programmes of learning and an expanded exhibition schedule.

We are developing the educational component of our new web site to be launched this year. The RSC will make use of appropriate new technologies to disseminate its work in many different ways to its many audiences.

We can also use our knowledge of theatre techniques to help in other aspects of learning: classroom teaching techniques for subjects other than drama or English, including management and personnel issues.

Not all of these programmes are available all the time, and not all of them are yet in place. However, if you are interested in pursuing any of these options, the telephone numbers and e-mail addresses are as follows:

For information on general education activities contact the Education Administrator, Sarah Keevill, on **01789 403462**, or e-mail her on **sarah.keevill @rsc.org.uk.**

To find out about backstage tours, please contact our Tour Manager, Anne Tippett on **01789 403405**, or e-mail her on **theatre.tours@rsc.org.uk.**

STAY IN TOUCH

For up-to-date news on the RSC, our productions and education work visit the RSC's official web site: **www.rsc.org.uk**. Information on RSC performances is also available on Teletext

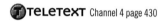 TELETEXT Channel 4 page 430

RSC MEMBERSHIP

Become an RSC Member and receive advance information and priority booking plus other exclusive benefits. Call our membership team on **01789 403440** for details of the various packages available, including UK membership, overseas, groups and education memberships. A free mailing list for those working in education is also available.

This production of *The Island Princess* was first performed by the Royal Shakespeare Company in the Swan Theatre, Stratford-upon-Avon, on 26 June 2002. The original cast was as follows:

Sasha Behar	Quisara
Claire Benedict	Quisana
Paul Bhattacharjee	Governor of Ternata
Vincent Brimble	Keeper
Antony Byrne	Pyniero
Billy Carter	Soza
Shelley Conn	Panura
Joe Dixon	King of Bakam
Jamie Glover	Armusia
Sean Hannaway	Captain
Ben Hicks	Emanuel
Michael Matus	King of Tidore
Keith Osborn	Christophero
David Rintoul	Ruy Dias
Avin Shah	King of Syana
James Tucker	Pedro

Directed by	**Gregory Doran**
Designed by	**Niki Turner**
Lighting designed by	**Wayne Dowdeswell**
Music by	**Adrian Lee**
Fights by	**Terry King**
Sound designed by	**Martin Slavin**
Music Director	**Adrian Lee**
Casting Director	**Carrie Hilton**
Associate Director	**Heather Davies**
Production Managers	**Stuart Gibbons and Mark Graham**
Costume Supervisor	**Janet Bench**
Dialect Coach	**Jeannette Nelson**
Company voice work by	**Andrew Wade and Jeannette Nelson**
Company Manager	**Jondon**

Stage Manager	**Leighton Vickers**
Deputy Stage Manager	**Amanda McCaffrey**
Assistant Stage Manager	**Christina Papaspyrou**

Gamelan players:	**Sunetra Fernando, James Jones, Adrian Lee, Michael Tubbs, Edward Watson**

This production was sponsored in Stratford-upon-Avon by

CONTENTS

PLAYS FOR A MONEY-GET, MECHANIC AGE

In his *An Expostulation with Inigo Jones,* Ben Jonson quarrels with Jones about the growing supremacy of scenery and stage effects over the spoken text, in the masques they produced together at court.

> Pack with your peddling poetry to the stage,
> This is a money-get, mechanic age.

The stage, unlike the court where the masques were held, was a place to go and use your eyes and your ears, a place where language had primacy, where you went to hear a play.

The stages of the Rose and the Globe needed no scenery, that would be conjured by words, words spoken by the actor standing in the centre of a circle of ears. The Swan Theatre in Stratford reproduces just such a relationship between actor and audience: vital, immediate and dangerous.

Since the Swan opened in 1986, we have done many plays from Shakespeare's time, all Jonson's major comedies (though none of his tragedies), all the major pays of Marlowe and Webster, as well as plays by Middleton and Ford, Kyd, Tourneur, Heywood and even Shirley and Broome. This season, I have chosen plays with which audiences are likely to be less familiar and which reflect something of the range of the drama of the period, from City Comedy to Revenge Tragedy and much in between.

I've included *Edward III*, recently canonized from the Shakespeare Apocrypha; *The Malcontent* by the unjustly neglected John Marston (this is his RSC debut); Massinger's magnificent *The Roman Actor* (Adrian Noble directed the only other Massinger play we've done, *A New Way to Pay Old Debts* at The Other Place in 1983); *Eastward Ho!*, a collaboration by Jonson, Marston and George Chapman; and finally, representing the popular genre of travel plays, a discovery, *The Island Princess* set in the Spice Islands and written by John Fletcher (who collaborated with Shakespeare on *Henry VIII or All Is True,* which I directed in the Swan in 1996).

This season is unusual not just because of the concentration on these lesser known plays from the repertoire, but because this is the first time we have explored these works with a dedicated ensemble company of 28 actors, who will perform all five plays in close repertoire. The Swan Theatre allows us to achieve this turnover very swiftly.

Though we have often had very large and elaborate scenery in the Swan, it works perfectly well without any; allowing all the flexibility and fluidity of Shakespeare's theatre. Basically very little set is needed for any of these plays and without much scenery of course we can achieve a much faster turnaround of plays and spend more time rehearsing in the space where we'll perform. So we have decided to work faster than usual in order to achieve a full repertoire by midsummer. And who knows, perhaps other things will be released by working all together at this pace, a different dynamic, a closer collaborative spirit? These days we are used to discussing character and motivation at length in rehearsal. Neither of these words would have been understood by an actor in Shakespeare's day. The text was the character. And as far as we can tell there was very little rehearsal at all. Nowadays we are used to letting things cook more slowly in rehearsal, so let's see what more of a stir-fry mentality can achieve!

It's a punishing schedule, but our workloads look light in comparison with the actors in Shakespeare's day. In the 1594-5 season at the Rose Theatre, according to Philip Henslowe's Diary, the Lord Admiral's Men performed 38 plays, 21 of which were new! It's a fascinating statistic and one which reflects the audience's appetite for drama in that 'money-get mechanic age'. Jonson's phrase could well describe our own time, and perhaps begins to suggest why the plays of Shakespeare and his contemporaries echo and resonate so profoundly with our own.

GREGORY DORAN

March 2002

INTRODUCTION

When directors and critics want to find a connection between Jacobean colonialism and the Jacobean stage, they generally turn to Shakespeare's *Tempest*, seeing in the fraught relationship between Prospero and Caliban that of colonist and colonised, and reading this relationship – cued both by Shakespeare's source materials and by Ariel's reference to the 'still-vex'd Bermoothes' – in the context of the plantation of America and the West Indies. Yet Shakespeare was not the only English Renaissance playwright to portray colonial relations, nor was the New World the only site of colonial and commercial exploitation by Europeans in the early seventeenth-century.

According to the first printed edition, John Fletcher's 1621 romantic tragi-comedy, *The Island Princess*, is set in 'India', but this was a sweeping, inexact term at the time, encompassing both west (America and the West Indies) and east (India and beyond): the play's specific setting is two islands in the Moluccan archipelago situated to the south of the Philippines in what is now Indonesia – better known in Fletcher's day as the 'Spice Islands' – which had borne the brunt of imperial struggle for well over a century by the time the play was written. *The Island Princess* – the first play on the English stage to be set in the East Indies – engages with, represents, and parodies the motivations for colonial adventure and the experiences of European voyagers as they come to terms with, and seek to impose their control over, alien cultures. In the process, it offers audiences now a unique and entertaining point of access to the Jacobean mindset.

The Island Princess was first performed at Court on 26th December 1621. Like most of the plays in the 'Beaumont and Fletcher' canon (now known to comprise a couple of plays by Francis Beaumont, a handful by the team of Beaumont and Fletcher, and the bulk by Fletcher either on his own or, more frequently, in collaboration with others, principally Philip Massinger), it was not published until 1647, when the publisher Humphrey Moseley assembled his Folio edition. *The Island Princess* is one of the 'solo' plays in the collection, written when Fletcher was at the height of his career as principal playwright for the King's Men, London's leading acting company. The play's success was marked by its reappearance on the stage after the Civil War in a slightly altered version which Samuel Pepys saw several times in 1669 and which 'pleased [him] better and better every time'; it was again revived twenty years later in a version by Nahum Tate (best-known for his happy-ending adaptation of *King Lear*); and appeared once more, ten years on, heavily cut and reworked by Peter Motteux as an opera. Thereafter it disappeared from the stage. The

Victorians didn't know what to do with Fletcher – there was too much innuendo, not enough 'moral' behaviour – and few of the plays survived in the theatre into the twentieth century. Greg Doran's 2002 production for the RSC is, to the best of my knowledge, the first full professional production since Tate and is certainly the first production of the original version of the play for three hundred and seventy-odd years.

The Island Princess is a hugely entertaining, emotionally-charged, comic swash-buckler of a play, set in an exotic location and sustained by a series of explosive events, including the burning down of one town and the destruction by bombardment of another. The centre of attention is Quisara, princess of the island of Tidore, and her various suitors, who include princes from neigh-bouring islands – including the villainous Governor of Ternata – and two Portuguese colonists, Ruy Dias and Armusia. Quisara embodies in herself – in the quintessential metaphor of colonialism – the riches and beauty of her land, and she impressively plays all the men off against each other, eliding her allegiances and – in an early modern take on medieval romance – demanding heroic action as proof of desire and worth, action which the staid Ruy Dias is too slow to undertake, leaving him to watch, frustrated, as his recently-arrived, déclassé countryman Armusia storms the Governor's prison, frees Quisara's captive brother, and claims her hand.

Giles Milton's *Nathaniel's Nutmeg* has recently provided an engaging account of European attempts to exploit the apparently boundless resources of the 'Spice Islands' in a time at which considerable medicinal as well as culinary properties had been attributed to spices such as pepper, nutmeg and cloves; and he demonstrates some of the ways in which the European desire for what these islands had to offer went beyond the question of immediate commercial gain. The dispute over the Moluccas had in fact been central to the struggle for global dominance which had been triggered by Balboa's first sighting of the Pacific and the resultant realisation that the treaty established after Columbus – which had with glorious presumption divided the known world between Portugal and Castile – had inadequately demarcated the eastern hemisphere and thus left the question of western 'ownership' of the east awkwardly open, inspiring (according to Jerry Brotton) 'not only the first complete circum-navigation of the globe' – that of Magellan – but also the establishing of 'the contours of a recognizably modern global image of the world.' These tiny, feuding, fecund islands, then, had already had a powerful impact on western culture. But why would an English dramatist writing a play in 1621 turn to the Moluccas as the location for his dramatic action?

The answer lies in the English attempt to muscle in, late in the day, on the commercial potential of the Moluccas. The Iberian struggle over the islands had been resolved in 1529 in favour of the Portuguese, but the following decades saw their power wane, and the English arrived at the nadir of Portuguese imperial dreams. In 1578, the young King of Portugal was killed, along with thousands of his soldiers, at the conclusion of an incompetent crusade against the Moors. A year or so later, Sir Francis Drake appeared in the Islands, unsettling the Portuguese commander by bringing him news of his king's death. Drake's return to London was greeted with a hysteria which marked both the ostensible fulfilment of long-held English dreams of riches from the East and a tacit acknowledgement of the belatedness of the endeavour. But the Dutch had already filled the gap left by the Portuguese and were uninclined to allow the late-arriving English to displace them. By the mid-1610s, the rivalry had become both overt and ferocious, and by the time of the Court performance of *The Island Princess* in 1621, the very existence of the East India Company was under threat. Within a little over a year, things came to a bloody head with the massacre of English merchants by the Dutch at Amboyna, a catastrophe which abruptly curtailed English interest in the Spice Islands. In this context, then, the play – though ostensibly set back at the time of Portuguese control over the Moluccas – can be seen to be engaging with current and troublesome events.

Michael Neill has shown that we need to read the Portuguese rivals, Ruy Dias and Armusia, at least in part as representing the conflicting claims and identities of the Dutch and the English in their struggle for the Spice Islands. Armusia can be read, as Shankar Raman has suggested, as a version of Sir Francis Drake, representing the ideal English knight-merchant in contrast to the slow, cautious, aristocratic figure of Ruy Dias, who is representative instead of the established Dutch colonists in the current struggle. Ruy Dias's 'coldness' loses him the princess, even though she claims to love him, whereas Armusia's decisiveness and instant action wins the day. Such was the shape of the English fantasy of a Spice Island succession that never unfolded.

Armusia's achievement in claiming Quisara's hand is, of course, fraught with problems, not the least of which is religion. The play broaches not only the colonial struggle to maintain control over the islanders but also the question of miscegenation, the (to the Jacobean audience) problematic desire of the Europeans for the native Other. In the process, it invokes the ever-present danger that the conversion process might work in reverse – that, rather than preaching the true faith, Europeans might instead succumb to the seductive power of strange places, strange women and strange faiths. It is not so far from Armusia's first awestruck delight at his first sight of the islands –

> The very rivers as we floate along,
> Throw up their pearles, and curle their heads to court us;
> The bowels of the earth swell with the births
> Of thousand unknowne gems, and thousand riches

– to his first, sexually-charged response to *The Island Princess* – 'a rare woman, sweet and goodly / An admirable forme' – to the situation in which he finds himself when she announces that she expects him, as her fiancé, to convert to her faith: 'change your religion, / And be of one beleefe with me. . . . / Worship our Gods, renounce the faith that you were bred in,' adding, with typical Fletcherian nonchalance and mischievousness, ' 'Tis easily done.'

The Island Princess thus brings into play perhaps the most difficult question of all for Jacobeans, that of the place of Christianity within a rapidly expanding and heterogeneous world, and it provides an uncomfortable resolution in which the female protagonist is converted but her brother the King remains only 'halfe perswaded' by Christianity's claims. The religious danger depicted in the play, despite the fact that the local religion is represented for the most part as generically heathen, is clearly associated with Islam, and in his dual role as crafty native and 'Moor' priest, the Governor of Ternata embodies the Moslem threat. The term 'Moor' had both racial and religious implications for Jacobeans: if a Christian converted to Islam, it was as if a racial transformation had also happened – a Christian 'turned Turk' or 'turned Moor' – and at the height of his rant against Quisara's religion (about which he is clearly very vague), Armusia refers to her 'maumet' gods, a term which had come to mean 'idol' or just 'doll' by this time, but which originally derived from the name Muhammed. In Armusia's over-the-top resistance to Quisara's faith can be heard Europe's fear of Islam and all the ignorance and bigotry that accompanied (and still accompanies) it.

In this context, the speech the Governor makes, in his 'Moor priest' disguise, to the King of Tidore, warning the King about the true intentions of the colonising Portuguese, is all the more remarkable, describing as it does the initial dynamic of colonial power:

> These men came hether as my vision tels me,
> Poore, weatherbeaten, almost lost, starv'd, feebled,
> Their vessels like themselves, most miserable;
> Made a long sute for traffique, and for comfort,
> To vent their childrens toyes, cure their diseases:
> They had their sute, they landed, and too th'rate
> Grew rich and powerfull, suckt the fat, and freedome
> Of this most blessed Isle, taught her to tremble;
> Witnesse the Castle here, the Cittadell,
> They have clapt upon the necke of your Tidore,
> This happy town, till that she knew these strangers,
> To check her when she's jolly. . . .
> Though you be pleas'd to glorifie that fortune,
> And thinke these strangers Gods, take heed I say,
> I find it but a hansome preparation,
> A faire fac'd Prologue to a further mischiefe.

blessed Isle

This is an astonishingly frank account – which must have been familiar to any in the audience who had read colonial narratives and which bears comparison with Caliban's complaints about the way in which Prospero took control of his island – of the process by which the European colonists, arriving initially hungry and exhausted after months at sea, gradually established their control over the locals who at first helped them. And although it is spoken by the conniving Governor – who tells us in an aside that his 'maine end is to advise . . . a generall ruine' – it is nonetheless a powerful exposé of the underhand processes of colonisation and stands in direct contrast to Armusia's initial celebration of the openness and availability of local resources to the English adventurer.

The Island Princess, then, offers us access into the complex mental processes involved in early voyaging and into Jacobean attitudes to sex, to inter-racial marriage, to other regions and to other religions; and it deploys its exotic setting in order simultaneously to mythologise and to expose English aspirations for commercial and colonial expansion in the Far East. In its depictions of fired cities and artillery bombardments, it demonstrates the way in which Europeans deployed their technological superiority to enforce their commercial will; at the same time, through the rivalry between Ruy Dias and Armusia, it also shows the ferocity of the competition amongst the Europeans themselves for power in the East and the tenuousness of England's claims for, and hold on, such power. And above all it offers us Quisara, the first portrayal of an Indonesian woman on the English stage and a gloriously complex portrayal at that, as she negotiates her way through the fraught terrain of sexual and political competition that frames her, for the play's first audiences, as an object of awe, of desire, and of fear.

GORDON MCMULLAN
Reader in English, King's College London

CHARACTERS

Quisara
the Island Princess, sister to the King of Thebes

Quisana
aunt to the Princess

Governor of Ternata
an ill man

Keeper

Pyniero
nephew to Ruy Dias, a merry Captain

Soza   Emanuel
companions to Armusia and his valiant followers

Panura
waiting woman to the Princess Quisara

King of Tidore

King of Bakam   King of Syana
suitors to the Princess Quisara

Armusia
a noble daring Portuguese, in love with the Princess

Captain

Christophero   Pedro
soldiers and friends to Pyniero

Ruy Dias
a Captain of Portugal, also suitor to the Princess

THE ISLAND PRINCESS

(handwritten annotations at top)
Gov of Ternata
captured King of Tidore
Quisara is Tidore's sister

ACT ONE

SCENE ONE

A bell rings
Enter Pyniero, Christophero, and Pedro

Pyniero	Open the Ports, and see the watch reliev'd,
	And let the guards be careful of their business,
	Their vigilant eyes fix'd on these Islanders.
	They're crafty souls, believe me Gentlemen.
	Their late attempt, which is too fresh amongst us,
	In which against all arms, and honesty,
	The Governor of Ternata made surprise
	Of our confederate, the King of Tidore
	As for his recreation he was rowing
	Between the Islands, bids us be circumspect. *p.7*

(handwritten left margin: Caliban / native / creatures / must be / alert.)

Christophero	It was a mischief suddenly imagin'd,
	And as soon done; that Governor's a fierce knave,
	Unfaithful as he is fierce too, there's no trusting;
	But I wonder much how such poor and base pleasure
	As tugging at an oar should become Princes.

Pyniero	Base breedings love base pleasure;
	They take as much delight in rowing,
	As we Portugals, or the Spanish do in riding,
	The French in Courtship, or the dancing English,
	In carrying a fair presence.

Pedro	He was strangely taken;
	But where no faith is, there's no trust; he has paid for't.
	His sister yet, the fair and noble Quisara,
	Has showed a noble mind to her afflicted brother,

The nobler still it appears,
Because his ruin styles her absolute
And his imprisonment adds to her profit.
Feeling all this, which makes all men admire her,
Yet has she made diverse treaties
For her brother's freedom, if wealth or honour –

Pyniero Peace, peace, you are fool'd sir;
They that observe her close shall find her nature,
Which I doubt mainly will not prove so excellent;
She is a Princess, and she must be fair,
That's the prerogative of being royal:
Let her want eyes and nose, she must be beauteous,
And she must know it too, and the use of it,
And people must believe it, they are damn'd else:
Why, all the neighbour Princes are mad for her.

Christophero Is she not fair then?

Pyniero   But her hopes are fairer,
And there's a haughty Master, the King of Bakam,
That lofty sir, that speaks far more, and louder,
In his own commendations than a Cannon:
He is strucken dumb with her.

Pedro   Beshrew me she is a sweet one.

Pyniero And there's that hopeful man of Syana,
That sprightly fellow, he that's wise and temperate,
He is a lover too.

Christophero   Would I were worth her looking:
For by my life I hold her a complete one,
The very Sun I think, affects her sweetness,
And dares not as he does to all else, dye it
Into his tawny Livery.

Pyniero   She dares not see the Sun,
But keeps herself at distance from his kisses,

07 九 一 33

12 21 38

17 26 31 43

五 31 ..

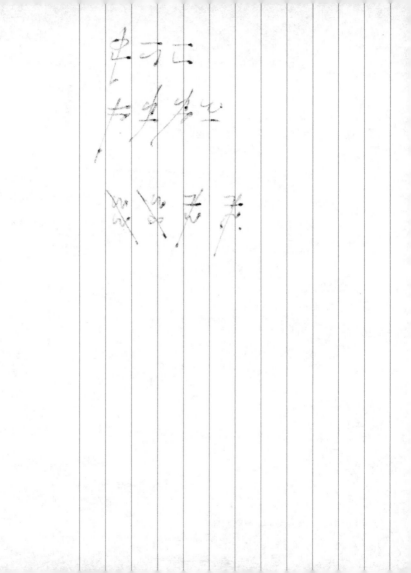

Gvr of Ternata captures King &
ACT ONE, SCENE ONE   5
is in love with King's sister

And wears her complexion in a case, let him but like it
A week or two, or three, she would look like a Lion;
But the main sport on't is, or rather wonder,
The Governor of Ternata, her mortal enemy,
He that has catcht her brother King is struck too,
He has admittance, and solicits hourly,
Now if he have the trick –

Pedro   What trick?

Pyniero   The true one,
To take her too, if he be but skill'd in bat-fowling,
And lime his bush right.

Christophero   I'll be hang'd when that hits,
For 'tis not a compell'd or forc'd affection,
That must take her, I guess her stout and virtuous.
But where's your uncle sir, our valiant Captain,
The brave Ruy Dias all this while?

Pyniero   Aye marry,
He is amongst 'em too.

Pedro   A Lover?

Pyniero   Nay,
I know not that, but sure he stands in favour,
Or would stand stiffly, he is no Portugal else.

Christophero   The voice says in good favour, in the list too
Of the privy wooers; how cunningly of late
I have observ'd him, and how privately
He has stol'n at all hours from us, and how readily
He has feign'd a business to bid the Fort farewell
For five or six days, or a month together,
Sure there is something –

Pyniero   Yes, yes, there is a thing in't,
A thing would make the best on's all dance after it;

A dainty thing; Lord how this uncle of mine
Has read to me, and rated me for wenching,
And told me in what desperate case 'twould leave me,
And how 'twould stew my bones.

Pedro   You car'd not for it.

Pyniero   I'faith, no. Danger is a Soldier's honour;
             But that this man, this herb of Grace, Ruy Dias,
             This father of our faculties should slip thus,
             For sure he is a-ferreting, that he
             That would drink nothing to depress the spirit,
             But milk and water, should tickle,
             And have a love mange on him.

Christophero   'Tis in him sir
             But honourable courtship, and becomes his rank too.

Pyniero   In me 'twere abominable Lechery, or would be,
             For when our thoughts are on't, and miss their level,
             We must hit something.

Pedro   Well, 'is a noble Gentleman,
             And if he be a suitor, may he speed in't.

Pyniero   Let him alone, our family ne'er fail'd yet.

Christophero Our mad Lieutenant still, merry Pyniero,
             Thus would he do if the Surgeon were searching of him.

Pedro   Especially if a warm wench had shot him.

Pyniero   But hark Christophero; come hither Pedro;
             When saw you our brave countryman Armusia?
             He that's arrived lately, and his gallants?
             A goodly fellow, and no doubt truly valiant.
             For he that dares come hither, dares fight anywhere.

Christophero I saw him not of late.

Pyniero	I love him,
	And by my troth would fain be inward with him;
	Pray let's go seek him.
Pedro	We'll attend you sir.
Pyniero	By that time we shall hear the burst of business.

Exeunt

SCENE TWO

Enter Ruy Dias, Quisara, Quisana and Panura

Quisara Aunt I much thank you for your courtesy,
And the fair liberty you still allow me,
Both of your house and service, though I be
A Princess, and by that Prerogative stand free,
And no ways bound to render up my actions,
Because no power above me can examine me;
Yet my dear brother being still a prisoner,
And many wand'ring eyes upon my ways,
Being left alone a Sea-mark, it behoves me
To use a little caution, and be circumspect.

Quisana You're wise and noble, Lady.

Quisara   Often Aunt
I resort hither, and privately to see you
It may be to converse with some I favour;
I would not have it known as oft, nor constru'd,
It stands not with my care.

Quisana   You speak most fairly,
For even our pure devotions are examin'd.

Quisara So made are men's minds now.

Ruy Dias	Or rather monstrous;
	They are thick dreams bred in fogs that know no fairness.
Quisana	Madam the house is yours, I am yours, pray use me,
	And at your service all I have lies prostrate;
	My care shall ever be to yield ye honour,
	And when your fame falls here, 'tis my fault Lady;
	A poor and simple banquet I have provided,
	Which if you please to honour with your presence –
Quisara	I thank ye Aunt, I shall be with you instantly,
	A few words with this Gentleman.
Quisana	I'll leave ye,
	And when you please retire, I'll wait upon you.

Exeunt Quisana and Panura

Quisara	Why, how now Captain, what, afraid to speak to me?
	A man of arms, and daunted with a Lady?
	Commanders have the power to parle with Princes.
Ruy Dias	Madam, the favours you have still showr'd on me,
	Which are so high above my means of merit,
	Strike me thus mute; you are my royal Mistress,
	And all my services that aim at honour,
	Take life from you, the Saint of my devotions;
	Pardon my wish, it is a fair ambition,
	And well becomes the man that honours you,
	I would I were of worth, a King I would be,
	A mighty King that might command affection,
	And bring a youth upon me might bewitch ye,
	And you a sweet soul'd Christian.
Quisara	Now you talk sir;
	You Portugals, though you be rugged Soldiers,
	Yet when you list to flatter, you are plain courtiers;
	And could you wish me Christian brave Ruy Dias?

Ruy Dias	At all the danger of my life great Lady,
	At all my hopes, at all –
Quisara	Pray ye stay a little,
	To what end runs your wish?
Ruy Dias	O glorious Lady,
	That I might – but I dare not speak.
Quisara	I dare then,
	That you might hope to marry me; nay blush not,
	An honourable end needs no excuse;
	And would you love me then?
Ruy Dias	My soul not dearer.
Quisara	Do some brave thing that may entice me that way,
	Some thing of such a meritorious goodness,
	Of such an unmatch'd nobleness, that I may know
	You have a power beyond ours that preserves you;
	'Tis not the person, nor the royal title,
	Nor wealth, nor glory that I look upon,
	That inward man I love that's lin'd with virtue.
	I have many Princes suitors, many great ones,
	Yet above these I love you; you are valiant,
	An active man, able to build a fortune;
	I do not say I dote, nor mean to marry,
	Only the hope is something may be done,
	That may compel my faith, and ask my freedom,
	And leave opinion fair.
Ruy Dias	Command dear Lady,
	And let the danger be as deep as hell,
	As direful to attempt –
Quisara	Y'are too sudden.
	A thousand uses for your forward spirit
	Ye may find daily that may advance ye,
	Forced smiles reward poor dangers; you are a Soldier,

sudden

I would not talk so else, and I love a Soldier,
Yet for all these which are but women's follies,
You may do what you please, I shall still know ye;
And though ye wear no sword –

Ruy Dias   Excellent Lady,
When I grow so cold, and disgrace my nation,
That from their hardy nurses suck adventures,
'Twere fit I wore a Tombstone; you have read to me
The story of your favour, if I mistake it,
Or grow a truant in the study of it,
A great correction Lady –

Quisara   Let's to th' banquet,
And have some merrier talk, and then to Court,
Where I give audience to my general Suitors;
Pray heaven any woman's wit hold; there brave Captain,
You may perchance meet something that may startle ye;
I'll say no more, come be not sad – I love ye.

mystery

she down'd   *Exeunt*

SCENE THREE

Enter Pyniero, Armusia, Soza, Christophero, and Emanuel

Pyniero   You are welcome gentlemen, most worthy welcome,
And know there's nothing in our power may serve ye,
But you may freely challenge.

Armusia   Sir we thank ye,
And rest your servants too.

Pyniero   Ye are worthy Portugals,
You show the bravery of your minds and spirits;
The nature of our country too, that brings forth

blessed Islands
Inhumate Islands

Stirring, unwearied souls to seek adventures;
Minds never satisfied with search of honour:
Where time is, and the sun gives light, brave countrymen,
Our names are known, new worlds disclose their riches,
Their beauties, and their prides to our embraces;
And we, the first of nations, find these wonders.

Theodoruka

Armusia   These noble thoughts sir, have entic'd us forward,
And minds unapt for ease to see these miracles,
In which we find report a poor relater;
We are arriv'd among these blessed Islands,   *Forhwale*
Where every wind that rises blows perfumes,
And every breath of air is like an Incense:
The treasure of the Sun dwells here, each tree   *Golden World*
As if it envied the old Paradise,
Strives to bring forth immortal fruit; the spices
Renewing nature, though not deifying,
And when that falls by time, scorning the earth,
The sullen earth, should taint or suck their beauties,
But as we dreamt, for ever so preserve us: *Caliban*
Nothing we see, but breeds an admiration;
The very rivers as we float along,
Throw up their pearls, and curl their heads to court us;
The bowels of the earth swell with the births
Of thousand unknown gems, and thousand riches;
Nothing that bears a life, but brings a treasure;   *Caliban*
The people they show brave too, civil manner'd,
Proportioned like the Masters of great minds,   *admiring*
The women which I wonder at –

riches

Pyniero   Ye speak well.

Armusia   Of delicate aspects, fair, clearly beauteous,
And to that admiration, sweet and courteous.

Pyniero   And is not that a good thing? brave Armusia
You never saw the court before?

Armusia handwritten: Armusia wonders at dopes, like

Merchant Venice handwritten

Armusia   No certain,
But that I see a (wonder) too, all excellent,
The Government exact.

Christophero   Ye shall see anon,
That that will make ye start indeed, such beauties,
Such riches, and such form.

Soza   We are fire already;
The wealthy Magazine of nature sure
Inhabits here.

Enter Bakam, Syana, Governor
[The Gallants talk apart]

Armusia   These sure are all (Islanders.)

Pyniero   Yes, and great Princes too, and lusty lovers.

Armusia   They are goodly persons; what might he be signior
That bears so proud a state?

Pyniero   King of Bakam,
A fellow that (farts) terror.

Emanuel   He looks highly,
Sure he was begot o'th'top of a steeple.

Christophero   It may well be,
For you shall hear him ring anon.

Pyniero   That is Syana,
And a brave temper'd fellow, and more valiant.

Soza   What rugged face is that?

Pyniero   That's the great Governor,
The man surpris'd our friend, I told ye of him.

Armusia   Has dangerous eyes.

Pyniero   A perilous thief, and subtle.

Iron

Christophero	And to that subtlety a heart of Iron.
Pyniero	Yet the young Lady makes it melt.
Armusia	They start all, And thunder in the eyes.
Bakam	Away ye poor ones, Am I in competition with such bubbles? My virtue, and my name rank'd with such trifles?
Syana	Ye speak loud.
Bakam	Young man, I will speak louder; Can any man but I, deserve her favour, You petty Princes?

Princes fly at one another

Pyniero	He will put 'em all in his pocket.
Syana	Thou proud mad thing be not so full of glory, So full of vanity.
Bakam	How? I condemn thee, And that fort-keeping fellow.
Pyniero	How the dog looks, The bandog Governor!
Governor	Ha, why?
Bakam	Away thing, And keep your rank with those that fit your royalty: – Call out the Princess.
Governor	Dost thou know me bladder, Thou insolent impostume?
Bakam	I despise thee;
Governor	Art thou acquainted with my nature, baby?

With my revenge for injuries? dar'st thou hold me
So far behind thy file, I cannot reach thee?
What canst thou merit?

Bakam   Merit? I am above it;
I am equal with all honours, all achievements,
And what is great and worthy.
'Tis in my power now to despise such wretches,
To look upon ye slightly, and neglect ye,
And but she deigns at some hours to remember ye,
And people have bestowed some titles on ye,
I should forget your names –

Syana   Mercy of me;
What a blown fool has self affection
Made of this fellow? – did not the Queen your mother,
Long for bellows and bagpipes when she was great with ye
She brought forth such a windy birth?

Governor   'Tis ten to one
She ate a Drum, and was deliver'd of a bell,

Syana   Faith talk a little handsomer, we are Princes;
Talk wiser, 'twill well become your mightiness;
Talk less, that men may think ye can do more.

Governor   Talk truth, that men may think ye are honest,
Or talk your self asleep, for I am weary of you.

Bakam   Why? I can talk and do.

Governor   That would do excellent.

Bakam   And tell you only I deserve the Princess,
And make good only I, if you dare, you sir,
Or you Syana's Prince.

Pyniero   Here's a storm toward,
Methinks it sings already: to him Governor.

Governor	Here lies my proof. *Draws*
Syana	And mine.
Governor	I'll be short with ye, For these long arguments I was never good at.
Pyniero	How white the boaster looks!
Armusia	I see he lacks faith.

Enter Ruy Dias, Quisara, Quisana, Panura

Ruy Dias	For shame forbear great Princes, rule your angers, You violate the freedom of this place, The state and royalty –
Governor	He is well contented It seems, and so I have done.
Armusia	Is this she, signior?
Pyniero	This is the Princess sir.
Armusia	She is sweet and goodly, An admirable form, they have cause to jostle.
Quisara	You wrong me and my court, ye froward Princes; Comes your love wrapp'd in violence to seek us? Is't fit though you be great, my presence should be Stain'd, and polluted with your bloody rages? My privacies affrighted with your swords? He that loves me, loves my command; be temper'd, Or be no more what ye profess, my Servants.
Princes	We are calm as peace.
Armusia	What command she carries! And what a sparkling Majesty flies from her!
Quisara	'Tis not contention, Who loves me to my face best, or who can flatter most

[handwritten: Princess has noble spirit: requires an adventure]

Can carry me, he that deserves my favour,
And will enjoy what I bring, love and Majesty,
Must win me with his worth.

Princes   But show the way.

Quisara   And will: and then show you
A will to tread the way, I'll say ye are worthy.

Pyniero   What task now will she turn these hot youths to?
By this hand I love her a little now.

Quisara   'Tis not unknown to you
I had a royal brother, now miserable,
And Prisoner to that man; if I were ambitious,
There he should lie his miseries upon him:
If I were covetous, and my heart set on riches,
There he should die, his death would give me these;
For then stood I up absolute to do all;
Yet all these flattering shows of dignity,
These golden dreams of greatness cannot force me
To forget nature and my fair affection.
Therefore that man that would be known my lover,
Must be known his redeemer, and must bring him
Either alive or dead to my embraces,
For even his bones I scorn shall feel such slavery,
Or seek another Mistress: 'twill be hard
To do this, wondrous hard, a great adventure,
Fit for a spirit of an equal greatness;
But being done, the reward is worthy of it.

[handwritten: Antonio did this ?]

Christophero   How they stand gaping all!

Quisara   [aside to Ruy Dias]   Ruy Dias cold?
Not fly like fire into it? – may be you doubt me,
He that shall do this is my husband, Princes;
By the bright heavens he is, by whose justice
I openly proclaim it; –
[aside] No stirring yet, no start into a bravery?

Ruy Dias	[*aside*] Madam, it may be, but being a main danger,
	Your Grace must give me leave to look about me,
	And take a little time, the cause will ask it,
	Great acts require great counsels.
Quisara	Take your pleasure,
	I fear ye Portugal.
Bakam	I'll raise an Army
	That shall bring back his Island, fort and all,
	And fix it here.
Governor	How long will this be doing?
	You should have begun in your Grandfather's days.
Syana	What may be,
	And what my power can promise noblest Lady,
	My will I am sure stands fair.
Quisara	Fair be your fortune,
	Few promises are best, and fair performance.
Governor	These cannot do, their power and arts are weak ones.
	'Tis in my will, I have this King your brother,
	He is my prisoner, I accept your proffer,
	And bless the fair occasion that achiev'd him:
	I love ye, and I honour ye, but speak
	Whether alive or dead he shall be rend'red,
	And see how readily, how in an instant,
	Quick as your wishes Lady –
Quisara	No, I scorn ye,
	You and your courtesy; I hate your love sir;
	And ere I would so basely win his liberty,
	I would study to forget he was my brother;
	By force he was taken; he that shall enjoy me,
	Shall fetch him back by force, or never know me.
Pyniero	As I live, a rare wench.
Armusia	She has a noble spirit.

Governor	By force?
Quisara	Yes sir by force, and make you glad too To let him go.
Governor	How? You may look nobler on me, And think me no such boy; by force he must not, For your love much may be.
Quisara	Put up your passion, And pack ye home; I say, by force and suddenly. He lies there till he rots else, although I love him Most tenderly and dearly, as a brother, And out of these respects would joy to see him; Yet to receive him as thy courtesy, With all the honour thou couldst add unto him From his hands that most hates him, I had rather See him far sunk i'th' earth, and there forget him.
Pyniero	Your hopes are gelt good, Governor.
Armusia	A rare woman.
Governor	Lady, I'll pull this pride, I'll quench this bravery, And turn your glorious scorn to tears and howlings; I will proud Princess; this neglect of me Shall make thy brother King most miserable; Shall turn him into curses 'gainst thy cruelty: For where before I us'd him like a King, And did those Royal Offices unto him, Now he shall lie a sad lump in a dungeon, Darkness and ling'ring death for his companions; And let me see who dare attempt his rescue, What desperate fool look toward it; farewell, And when thou know'st him thus, lament thy follies, Nay I will make thee kneel to take my offer: Once more farewell, and put thy trust in puppets.

Exit

Quisara	If none dare undertake it, I'll live a mourner.
Bakam	You cannot want.
Syana	You must not.
Ruy Dias	'Tis most dangerous,

And wise men would proceed with care and counsel,
Yet some way would I knew –
Walk with me Gentlemen-

Exeunt. Manent Armusia, Soza, and Emanuel

Armusia	How do you like her spirit?
Soza	'Tis a clear one,

Clod with no dirty stuff, she is all pure honour,

Emanuel	The bravest wench I ever look'd upon,

And of the strongest parts, she is most fair,
Yet her mind such a mirror –

Armusia	What an action

Would this be to put forward on, what a glory,
And what an everlasting wealth to end it!
Methinks my soul is strangely raised.

Soza	To step into it,

Just while they think, and, ere they have determin'd,
To bring the King off.

Armusia	Things have been done as dangerous.
Emanuel	And prosper'd best when they were least consider'd.
Armusia	Bless me my hopes, and you my friends assist me.

None but our companions –

Soza	You deal wisely,

And if we shrink the name of slaves die with us.

Emanuel	Stay not for second thoughts.

Armusia   I am determined;
And though I lose, it shall be sung, I was valiant,
And my brave offer shall be turn'd to story,
Worthy the Princess' tongue. A boat that's all
That's unprovided, and habits like to merchants,
The rest we'll counsel as we go.

Soza   Away then,
Fortune looks fair on those who make haste to win her.

Festina lente

Exeunt

Armusia decides to
pursue Quisara

King in prison
gov is cruel

ACT TWO

SCENE ONE

Enter Keeper

Keeper   I have kept many a man, and many a great one,
Yet I confess, I ne'er saw before
A man of such a sufferance; he lies now
Where I would not lay my dog, for sure 'twould kill him;
It grieves me to see a mighty King sunk
O'th' sudden to the bottom of a dungeon,
Whither should we descend that are poor Rascals
If we had our desserts! 'Tis a strange wonder;
Load him with Irons, oppress him with contempts,
Which are the Governor's commands, give him nothing,
Or so little, to sustain life, 'tis next nothing;
They stir not him, he smiles upon his miseries.
He gives no ill words, curses, nor repines not,
Blames nothing, hopes in nothing we can hear of;
And in the midst of all these frights, fears nothing.
And he will sing, woo his afflictions,
And court 'em in sad airs, as if he would wed 'em.
And his voice so affects me, so delights me,
That it stirs me infinitely.

King appears, loaden with chains; his head, arms only above

[*apart*] Now hark and melt, for I am sure I shall;
Your allowance from the Governor,

                 [*Music. King sings. Gives food to the King*]

                        would it were more sir,
Or in my power to make it handsomer.

King   Do not transgress thy charge, I take his bounty,
       And Fortune, whilst I bear a mind contented,
       Not leaven'd with the glory I am fall'n from,
       Nor hang upon vain hopes, that may corrupt me,
       Thou art my slave, and I appear above thee.

Enter Governor

Keeper   The Governor himself.

Governor   What, at your banquet?
           And in such state, and with such a change of service?

King   Nature's no glutton sir, a little serves her.

Governor   The diet's wholesome then?

King   I beg no better.

Governor   A calm contented mind, give him less next;
           These full meals will oppress his health, his Grace
           Is of a tender and pure constitution,
           And such repletions –

King   Mock, mock, it moves not me sir,
       Thy mirths, as do thy mischiefs fly behind me.

Governor   Ye carry it handsomely, but tell me patience,
           Do not you curse the brave and royal Lady
           Your gracious sister? Do not you damn her pity,
           Damn twenty times a day and damn it seriously?
           Do not you swear aloud too, cry and kick?
           The very soul sweat in thee with the agony
           Of her contempt of me? couldst not thou eat her

cannibal   For being so injurious to thy fortune,
           Thy fair and happy fortune? couldst not thou wish her
           A whore, or that thou hadst had no sister?
           Spitting the general name out, and the nature;
           Blaspheming heaven for making such a mischief;
           For giving power to pride, and will to woman?

King   No Tyrant, no, I bless and love her for it; *Tyrant*
        And though her scorn of thee had laid upon me
        As many plagues as the corrupted air breeds,
        As many forms of death, as doubt can figure;
        Yet I should love her more still, and more honour her;
        All thou canst lay upon me, cannot bend me,
        No not the stroke of death, that I despise too:
        For if fear could possess me, thou hadst won me;
        And if she be not Mistress of this nature,
        She is none of mine, no kin, and I condemn her.

Governor   Are you so valiant sir?

King   Yes, and so fortunate;
        For he that holds his constancy still conquers;
        Hadst thou preserv'd me as a noble enemy,
        And as at first, made my restraint seem to me
        But only as the shadow of captivity,
        I had still spoke thee noble, still declar'd thee
        A valiant, great and worthy man, still lov'd thee,
        And still prefer'd thy fair love to my sister;
        But to compel this from me with a misery,
        A most inhuman, and unhandsome slavery –

Governor   You will relent for all this talk I fear not,
        And put your wits a-work again.

King   Do thy utmost,
        And e'en in all thy tortures I'll laugh at thee,
        I'll think thee no more valiant, but a villain;
        Nothing thou hast done brave, but like a thief,
        Achiev'd by craft, and kept by cruelty;
        Nothing thou canst deserve, thou art unhonest;
        Nor no way live to build a name, thou art barbarous.

Governor   [*to Keeper*]
        Down with him low enough, there let him murmur,
        And see his diet be so light and little,

barbarous

Like
measure
to
measure

He grow not thus high hearted on't: – I will cool ye,
And make ye cry for mercy, and be ready
To work my ends, and willingly; and your sister
Your scornful, cruel sister shall repent too,
And sue to me for grace. Give him no liberty,
But let his bands be doubled, his ease lessen'd;
Nothing his heart desires, but vex and torture him:
Let him not sleep, nothing that's dear to nature
Let him enjoy; yet take heed that he die not,
Keep him as near death, and as willing to embrace it,
But see he arrive not at it; I will humble him,
And her stout heart that stands on such defiance;
And let me see her champions that dare venture
Her high and mighty wooers; keep your guards close,
And as you love your lives be diligent,
And what I charge, observe.

Keeper   I shall be dutiful

Governor   I'll pull your courage King and all your bravery.

                                        Exit Governor and King

Keeper   As willingly he sunk down to his sorrows,
                  As some men to their sleeps.
                  But much I fear has found his tomb already,
                  He cannot last long, and when he's dead, he's free.

                                                        Exit

Armusia's plan to rescue the king

SCENE TWO
Prospero

Enter Armusia, Soza, Emanuel, like merchants, arm'd underneath

Armusia	Our prosperous passage was an omen to us, A lucky and a fair omen.
Both	We believe it.
Armusia	The sea and wind strove who should most befriend us, And as they favour'd our design and lov'd us, So led us forth: – where lies the boat that brought us?
Soza	Safe lodg'd within the Reeds, close by the Castle, That no eye can suspect, nor thought come near it. *like Venus*
Emanuel	But where have you been, brave sir?
Armusia	I have broke the Ice boys, I have begun the game, if fortune guide it: Suspectless have I travell'd all the town through, And in this Merchant's shape survey'd each place That may befriend us, got perfect knowledge Of where the prison is, and what power guards it.
Soza	These will be strong attempts.
Armusia	Courage is strong: What we began with policy, my dear friends, Let's end with manly force; there's no retiring, Unless it be with shame.
Emanuel	Shame his that hopes it.
Soza	Direct, and we have done, bring us to execute, And if we flinch, or fail –
Armusia	I am sure ye dare not. Then further know, and let no ear be near us That may be false.

Emanuel	Speak boldly on, sweet sir.
Armusia	Close by the prison where he keeps the King,
	I have hir'd a lodging, as a trading merchant,
	A Cellar to that too, to stow my wares in,
	The very wall of which joins to his store-house.
Soza	What of all this?
Armusia	Ye are dull, if ye apprehend not:
	Into that Cellar, elected friends, I have convey'd
	That that will make all shake, and smoke too.
Emanuel	Ha?
Armusia	My thoughts have not been idle, nor my practice:
	The fire I brought here with me shall do something,
	Shall burst into material flames, and bright ones,
	That all the Island shall stand wond'ring at it,
	As if they had been stricken with a Comet:
	Powder is ready, and enough to work it,
	The match is left a-fire; all hush'd, and lock'd close,
	No man suspecting what I am but Merchant:
	An hour hence, my brave friends, look for the fury,
	The fire to light us to our honour'd purpose,
	For by that time 'twill take.
Soza	What are our duties?
Armusia	When all are full of fear and fright, the Governor
	Out of his wits, to see the flames so imperious,
	Ready to turn to ashes all he worships,
	And all the people there to stop these ruins,
	No man regarding any private office;
	Then fly we to the prison suddenly.
Emanuel	Then to our swords and good hearts, I long for it.
Armusia	Certain we shall not find much opposition,
	But what is must be forced.

Soza	'Tis bravely cast sir,
	And surely too I hope.

Armusia   If the fire fail not,
And powder hold his nature, some must presently
Upon the first cry of the amazed people,
(For nothing will be mark'd then, but the misery)
Be ready with the boat upon an instant,
And then all's right and fair.

Emanuel   Bless us dear fortune.

Armusia   Let us be worthy of it in our courage,
And fortune must befriend us; come, all sever,
But keep still within sight, when the flame rises
Let's meet, and either do, or die.

Soza   So be it.

                                        Exeunt

Armusia allady gon to set kwig

SCENE THREE

Enter Governor and Captain

Governor   No Captain, for those troops we need 'em not,
The Town is strong enough to stand their furies;
Dost think they dare attempt?

Captain   May be by treaty
But sure by force they will not prove so forward.

Governor   No faith, I warrant thee, they know me well enough,
And know they have no child in hand to play with:
They know my nature too, I have bit some of 'em,
And to the bones, they have reason to remember me.
Well would I had this wench, for I must have her,

	She must be mine; [*The Train takes*]
	Hark what was that,
	That noise there? it went with a violence.
Captain	Some old wall belike sir, is fallen suddenly.
Within	Fire, fire.
Governor	I hear another tune, good Captain,
	It comes on fresher still, 'tis loud and fearful,
	Look up into the Town: [*Exit* Captain]
	how bright the air shows;
	Upon my life some sudden fire. *Bell rings*
	The bell too?
	I hear the noise more clear.

Enter Keeper

Keeper	Fire, fire.
Governor	Where, where?
Keeper	Suddenly taken in a Merchant's house sir,
	Fearful and high it blazes; – help good people.
	[*Exit*]
Governor	Pox o' their paper-houses, how they smother,
	They light like candles, how the roar still rises!

Enter Captain

Captain	Your Magazine's a-fire sir, help, help, suddenly,
	The Castle too is in danger, in much danger,
	All will be lost, get the people presently,
	And all that are your guard, and all help, all hands sir,
	Your wealth, your strength, is burnt else, the town
	perish'd;
	The Castle now begins to flame.

Governor   My soul shakes.
          Raise all the garrison, and bring 'em up.

                                        [*Exit Captain*]

          Oh I have lost all in one house, all my hopes:
          Buckets, more Buckets; fire, fire, fire.

                                                    Exit

                Enter Armusia and his company

Armusia   Let it flame on, and comely light it gives up
          To our discovery.

Soza   Hark, what a merry cry
          These hounds make! forward fairly,
          We are not seen in the mist, we are not noted.
          Away, away. Now if we lose our fortune –

                                          Exeunt

                    Enter Captain

Captain   More water, more water, all is consum'd else.

                                        Exit Captain

          Enter Armusia and his company breaking open a door

Armusia   So, thou art open: – keep the way clear
          Behind still. Now for the place.
          Sure this is it.
          Force ope the door –

                                    The King discover'd

                        A miserable creature!
          Yet by his manly face –

King   Why stare ye on me?
          You cannot put on faces to affright me:

In death I am a King still, and condemn ye:
Where is that Governor? methinks his manhood
Should be well pleas'd to see my Tragedy,
And come to bath his stern eyes in my sorrows;
Here's a throat, soldiers;
Come, see who can strike deepest.

Emanuel   Break the Chain there.

King   What does this mean?

Armusia   Come, talk of no Governors,
He has other business sir, put your legs forward,
And gather up your courage like a man,
We'll carry off your head else: we are friends,
And come to give your sorrows ease.

Soza   On bravely;
Delays may lose again.

                        Enter Captain and Keeper

Armusia   The Guard.

Soza   Upon 'em.

Armusia   Make speedy, and sure work.

                          [*Fight, and Captain and Keeper fly*]

Emanuel   They fly.

Armusia   Up with him,
And to the Boat; stand fast, now be speedy,
When this heat's past, we'll sing our History.
Away, like thoughts, sudden as desires, friends;
Now sacred chance be ours.

Soza   Pray when we have done sir.

                                                        Exeunt

Gov vows revenge

SCENE FOUR *thinks they*

Enter Governor, Captain, and Keeper *were his*
man

Governor   The fire is quench'd, but the mischief hangs still;
             The King's redeem'd and gone too; a trick, a damn'd one:
             Oh I am overtaken poorly, tamely.

Captain   Where were the guard that waited upon the prison?

Keeper   Most of 'em slain, yet some scap'd sir.

Governor   I am lost Captain,
             And all the world will laugh at this, and scorn me:
             Count me a heavy sleepy fool, a coward.
             Oh, I could tear my limbs, and knock my boy's brains
             'Gainst every post I meet; fool'd with a fire!

Captain   It was a crafty trick.

Governor   No, I was lazy,
             Confident sluggish lazy, had I but met 'em,
             And chang'd a dozen blows, I had forgiv'n 'em.
             By both these hands held up, and by that brightness
             That gilds the world with light, by all our worships,
             The hidden ebbs and flows of the blue Ocean,
             I will not rest; no mirth shall dwell upon me,
             Wine touch my mouth, nor any thing refresh me,
             Till I be wholly quit of this dishonour:
             Make ready my Barratos instantly,
             And what I shall intend –

Captain   We are your servants.

                                              Exeunt

Q and Ruy conspire to kill King

SCENE FIVE

Enter Quisara, Ruy Dias

Quisara   Never tell me: you never car'd to win me,
                 Never for my sake to attempt a deed,
                 Might draw me to a thought you sought my favour:
                 If not for love of me, for love of arms sir.
                 You might have stept out nobly, and made an offer,
                 As if you had intended something excellent,
                 Put on a forward face.

Ruy Dias   Dear Lady hold me –

Quisara   I hold ye, as I find ye, a faint servant.

Ruy Dias   By – I dare do –

Quisara   In a Lady's chamber.
                 I dare believe ye; there's no mortal danger:
                 Give me the man that dares do, to deserve that:
                 I thought you Portugals had been rare wonders,
                 The Lords of fate and fortune, I believ'd ye,
                 But well I see I am deceiv'd Ruy Dias,
                 And blame too late my much belief.

Ruy Dias   I am asham'd, Lady,
                 I was so dull, so stupid to your offer:
                 Now you have once more school'd me, I am right,
                 And something shall be thought on suddenly,
                 And put in act as soon, some preparation –

Quisara   And give it out?

Ruy Dias   Yes, Lady, and so great too;
                 In which, the noise of all my Countrymen –

Quisara   Those will do well, for they are all approv'd ones,
                 And though he be restor'd alive –

Ruy Dias	I have ye.
Quisara	For then we are both servants. *crafty*
Ruy Dias	I conceive ye,
	Good Madam give me leave to turn my fancies.
Quisara	Do, and make all things fit, and then I'll visit you.

Exit

Ruy Dias	My self, my cozen, and the Garrison,
	The neighbours of the out-Isles of our nation,
	Syana's strength, for I can humour him:
	And proud Bakamus, I shall deceive his glory –

A shout

What ringing sound of joy is this? whence comes it?
May be the Princes are in sport.

Enter Pyniero, Christophero

Pyniero	Where are ye?
Ruy Dias	Now Pyniero, what's the haste you seek me?
Pyniero	The King's come home again, the King.
Ruy Dias	The devil!
Pyniero	Nay sure he came a god's name home: he's return'd sir.
Christophero	And all this joy ye hear –
Ruy Dias	Who durst attempt him?
	The Princes are all here.
Christophero	Believe it sir, 'tis done, and done most bravely,
	And easily. What fortune have ye lost sir?
	What justice have ye now unto this Lady?

Prosper

Pyniero   How stands your claim? that ever man should be fool'd so,
When he should do and prosper; stand protesting,
Kissing the hand, and farting for a favour,
When he should be about his business sweating;
She bid you go, and pick'd you out a purpose,
And bid you fly: you have made a fair flight on't,
You have caught a goose.

Ruy Dias   How dare you thus molest me?
It cannot be.

A shout

Christophero   Hark how the general joy rings!

Pyniero   Have you your hearing left? is not that drunk too?
For if you had been sober, you had been wise sure.

Ruy Dias   Done? Who dares do?

Pyniero   It seems an honest fellow,
That has ended his Market before you be up.

Christophero   The shame on't 's a stranger too.

Pyniero   'Tis no shame,
He took her at her word, and tied the bargain,
Dealt like a man indeed, stood not demurring,
But clapp'd close to the cause, as he will do to the Lady:
He will get her with child too, ere you shall come to
                                know him,
Is it not brave, a gentleman scarce landed,
Scarce eating of the air here.

Ruy Dias   I am undone.

Pyniero   Like an Oyster:
You are undone as a man would undo an egg,
A hundred shames about ye.

Enter Quisara, Panura and Quisana

Quisara   Can it be possible,
A stranger that I have not known, not seen yet,
A man I never grac'd; O Captain, Captain,
What shall I do? I am betray'd by fortune,
It cannot be, it must not be.

Pyniero   It is Lady,
And by my faith a handsome Gentleman;
'Tis his poor Scholar's prize.

Quisara   Must I be given
Unto a man I never saw, ne'er spoke with,
I know not of what Nation!   *key?*

Pyniero   'Is a Portugal,
And of as good a pitch. He will be given to you Lady,
For he's given much to handsome flesh.

Quisara   Oh Ruy Dias,
This was your sloth, your sloth, your sloth Ruy Dias.

Pyniero   Your love sloth, Uncle, do you find it now?
You should have done at first, and faithfully:
And then the other had lied ready for ye;
Madam, the general joy comes.   *[A shout]*

Quisara   We must meet it –
But with what comfort

Enter Citizens carrying boughs, boys singing after them;
Then King, Armusia, Soza, Emanuel;
The Princes and train following

Quisara   Oh my dear brother what a joy runs through me,
To see you safe again, your self, and mighty,
What a blest day is this!

Suitors 8 haward

King	Rise up fair sister,
	I am not welcome till you have embraced me.
Ruy Dias	A general gladness sir flies through the City,
	And mirth possesses all to see your Grace arriv'd,
	Thus happily arrived again, and fairly;
	'Twas a brave venture whosoe'er put for it,
	A high and noble one, worthy much honour;
	And had it failed, we had not failed great sir,
	And in short time too to have forc'd the Governor,
	In spite of all his threats –
King	I thank ye Gentleman.
Ruy Dias	And all his subtleties to set you free,
	With all his heart and will too.
King	I know ye love me.
Pyniero	[*aside*] This had been good with something done before it,
	Now it sounds empty like a Barber's basin,
Bakam	I have an army sir, but that the Governor,
	The foolish fellow was a little provident,
	And wise in letting slip no time,
	That would have scoured him else,
	That would have rung him such a peal –
Pyniero	Yes backwards,
	To make dogs howl, I know thee to a farthing,
	Thy army's good for hawks, there's nothing but sheep's
	hearts in it.
Syana	I have done nothing sir, therefore I think it
	Convenient I say little what I purposed,
	And what my love intended.
King	I like your modesty:
	And thanks ye royal friends, I know it griev'd ye
	To know my misery; but this man Princes,

Kᴏᴋ Mᴇʀᴀᴋᴇ ᴀᴀᴀᴀᴀᴀᴀ

ACT TWO, SCENE FIVE 37

I must thank heartily indeed and truly,
For this man saw me in't, and redeemed me:
He look'd upon me sinking, and then caught me.
This sister this, this all man, this all valour,
This pious man.

Ruy Dias   [aside]   My countenance, it shames me;
One scarce arrived, not harden'd yet, not read
In dangers and great deeds, sea-sick, not season'd –
Oh I have boy'd myself.

King   This noble bulwark,
This launce and honour of our age and kingdom;
This that I never can reward, nor hope
To be once worthy of the name of friend to,
This, this man from the bowels of my sorrows
Has new begot my name, and once more made me:
Oh sister, if there may be thanks for this,
Or any thing near recompense invented –

Armusia   You are too noble sir, there is reward
Above my action too by millions:
A recompense so rich and glorious,
I durst not dream it mine, but that 'twas promised;
Before the face of heaven, I durst not hope it,
For nothing in the life of man, or merit,
It is so truly great, can else embrace.

King   O speak it, bless mine ears to hear it,
Make me a happy man, to know it may be,
For still methinks I am a prisoner,
And feel no liberty before I find it.

Armusia   Then know it is your sister, she is mine sir,
I claim her by her own word, and her honour;
It was her open promise to that man
That durst redeem ye; Beauty set me on,
And fortune crowns me fair, if she receive me.

King	Receive ye sir – why sister – ha – so backward,
	Stand as you knew me not, nor what he has ventured?
	My dearest sister.

Armusia	Good sir pardon me,
	There is a blushing modesty becomes her,
	That holds her back; women are nice to woo sir;
	I would not have her forced, give her fair liberty;
	For things compell'd and frighted of soft natures,
	Turn into fears, and fly from their own wishes.

King	Look on him my Quisara: such another,
	Oh all ye powers, so excellent in nature,
	In honour so abundant –

Quisara	I confess sir,
	Confess my word is past too, he has purchased;
	Yet good sir give me leave to think, but time
	To be acquainted with his worth and person;
	To make me fit to know it; we are both strangers.

King	Be certain in your way, no woman's doubles,
	Nor coy delays, you are his, and so assure it,
	Or cast from me and my remembrance ever;
	Respect your word, I know you will; come sister,
	Let's see what welcome you can give a prisoner,
	And what fair looks a friend: – Oh my most noble
	Princes, no discontents, but all be lusty,
	He that frowns this day is an open enemy:
	Thus in my arms my dear.

Armusia	You make me blush sir.

King	And now lead on – Our whole Court crowned with
	pleasure.

Ruy Dias	[apart] Madam, despair not, something shall be done yet,
	And suddenly and wisely.

Quisara	*[apart]*	O Ruy Dias.

Exeunt [all but Pyniero, Soza and Christophero]

Pyniero   Well he's a brave fellow, and he has deserv'd her richly,
And you have had your hands full I dare swear Gentlemen.

Soza   We have done something sir, if it hit right.

Christophero   The woman has no eyes else, nor no honesty;
So much I think.

Pyniero   Come, let's go bounce amongst 'em,
To the King's health, and my brave country-man's.
My uncle looks as though he were sick o'th' worms,
                                    friends.

Exeunt

ACT THREE

SCENE ONE

Enter Pyniero

Pyniero   Mine uncle haunts me up and down, looks melancholy,
Wondrous proof melancholy, sometimes swears,
Then whistles, starts, cries, and groans, as if he had the
Bots.
As to say truth, I think h'as little better,
And would fain speak; bids me good morrow at midnight,
And good night when 'tis noon, has something hovers
About his brains, that would fain find an issue,
But cannot out, or dares not:

[Enter Ruy Dias]

Still he follows;
Like an old Dog at a dead scent? Aye marry,
There was a sigh would a set a ship a sailing:
These winds of love and honour blow at all ends.
Now speak an 't be thy will: – good morrow Uncle.

Ruy Dias   Good morrow sir.

Pyniero   This is a new salute:
Sure h'as forgot me: this is purblind Cupid.

Ruy Dias   My nephew?

Pyniero   Yes sir, if I be not chang'd.

Ruy Dias   I would fain speak with you.

Pyniero	I would fain have ye sir,
	For to that end I stay.

Ruy Dias	You know I love ye,
	And I have lov'd you long, my dear Pyniero,
	Bred and supplied you –

Pyniero	Whither walks this Preamble?

Ruy Dias	You may remember, though I am but your Uncle,
	I had a father's care, a father's tenderness –

Pyniero	[aside] Sure he would wrap me into something
	Now suddenly; he winds me about so.

Ruy Dias	A father's diligence. O Pyniero –

Pyniero	Sir, what hangs upon you,
	What heavy weight oppresses ye?

Ruy Dias	Oh my best Nephew–

Pyniero	It may be ye fear her too, that disturbs ye,
	That she may fall her self, or be forc'd from ye.

Ruy Dias	She is ever true, but I undone for ever.
	Oh that Armusia, that new thing, that stranger,
	That flag stuck up to rob me of mine honour;
	That murd'ring chain shot at me from my Country;
	That goodly plague that I must court to kill me.

Pyniero	Now it comes flowing from him, I feared this –
	Has he not done a brave thing?

Ruy Dias	I must confess it nephew, must allow it,
	But that brave thing has undone me, has sunk me,
	Has trod me like a name in sand to nothing,
	Hangs betwixt hope and me, and threatens my ruin:
	And if he rise and blaze, farewell my fortune;

               And when that's set, where's thy advancement Cousin?
               That were a friend, that were a noble kinsman,
               That would consider these; that man were grateful;
               And he that durst do something here durst love me.

Pyniero   You say true, 'tis worth consideration,
               Your reasons are of weight, and mark me Uncle,
               For I'll be sudden, and to'th' purpose with you,
               Say this Armusia then were taken off,
               (As it may be easily done) how stands the woman?

Ruy Dias   She is mine forever;
               For she condemns his deed and him.

Pyniero   [*aside*]   Pox on him,
               Or if the single pox be not sufficient,
               The hogs, the dogs, and devils' pox possess him: –
               'Faith this Armusia stumbles me, 'is a brave fellow;
               And if he could be spared Uncle –

Ruy Dias   I must perish:
               Had he set up at any rest but this,
               Done any thing but what concern'd my credit,
               The everlasting losing of my worth –

Pyniero   [*aside*] I understand you now, who set you on too;
               I had a reasonable good opinion of the devil
               Till this hour; and I see he is a knave indeed,
               An arrant stinking knave, for now I smell him: –
               I'll see what may be done then, you shall know
               You have a kinsman, but no villain Uncle,
               Nor no betrayer of fair fame, I scorn it;
               I love and honour virtue; I must have
               Access unto the Lady to know her mind too,
               A good word from her mouth you know may stir me;
               A Lady's look at setting on –

Ruy Dias   You say well,
               Here Cousin, here's a Letter ready for you,

And you shall see how nobly she'll receive you,
And with what care direct.

Pynier   Farewell then Uncle,
After I have talked with her, I am your servant,
To make you honest if I can – [*aside*] else hate you. –
Pray ye no more compliments, my head is busy.

Exit Ruy Dias

Heaven bless me;
What a malicious soul does this man carry!
And to what scurvy things this love converts us!
What stinking things, and how sweetly they become us!
Murder's a moral virtue with these Lovers,
A special piece of Divinity I take it:
I may be mad, or violently drunk,
Which is a whelp of that litter; or I may be covetous,
And learn to murder men's estates, that's base too;
Or proud, but that's a Paradise to this;
Or envious, and sit eating of myself
At other's fortunes; I may lie, and damnably,
Beyond the patience of an honest hearer;
Cozen, cut purses, sit i'th' stocks for apples:
But when I am a lover, Lord have mercy,
These are poor pelting sins, or rather plagues;
Love and Ambition draw the devil's Coach.

Enter Quisana, and Panura

How now! Who are these? Oh my great Lady's followers,
Her riddle-founders, and her fortune-tellers,
Her readers of her love-lectures, her inflamers:
These doors I must pass through, I hope they are wide.
– Good day to your beauties: – [*aside*] how they take it
                                                    to 'em!
As if they were fair indeed.

Pyniera is saudanic

Quisana	Good morrow to you sir.
Pyniero	That's the old Hen, the brood-bird! how she bustles! How like an Inventory of Lechery she looks! – I beseech you, is the fair Princess stirring?
Panura	Yes marry is she sir. But somewhat private: have you a business with her?
Pyniero	Yes forsooth have I, and a serious business.
Panura	May not we know?
Pyniero	Yes, when you can keep counsel.
Panura	How prettily he looks! he's a soldier sure, His rudeness sits so handsomely upon him.
Quisana	A good blunt gentleman.
Pyniero	Yes marry am I: Yet for a push or two at sharp, an't please you –
Panura	My honest friend, you know not who you speak to: This is the Princess' Aunt.
Pyniero	I like her th' better: And she were her Mother, (Lady) or her grandmother, I am not so bashful but I can buckle with her.
Panura	Of what size is your business?
Pyniero	Of the long sixteens, And will make way I warrant ye.
Panura	How fine he talks!
Pyniero	Nay in troth I talk but coarsely, Lady, But I hold it comfortable for the understanding: – How fain they would draw me into ribaldry!
Panura	Why do you look so on me?

Pyniero   I presume you turn a key sweet beauty,
            And you another, gravity, under the Princess,

Quisana   Methinks he talks handsomely.

Pyniero   And truly.
            You look as if you kept my lady's secrets:
            Nay do not laugh, for I mean honestly: –
            How these young things tattle, when they get a toy
                                                    by th'end!
            Your gravity I guess to hear the ling'ring suits in love
                                                    dispos'd,
            Their sighs and sorrows in their proper place,
            You keep the ay-me office.

Quisana   [to Panura]   Prithee suffer him,
            For as I live he's a pretty fellow.
            I love to hear sometimes what men think of us:
            And 'tis deliver'd freely, 'tis no malice: –
            Proceed good honest man.

Pyniero   I will, good Madam.
            According to men's states you rate their dreams,
            And cast the Nativity of their desires,
            If he reward well, his dreams are Oracles;
            Your ancient Art yields you no little profit,
            For these ye milk by circumstance.

Quisana   Ye are cunning.

Pyniero   And as they oil ye, and advance your spindle,
            So you draw out the lines of love; your doors too,
            The doors of destiny, that men must pass through;
            These are fair places.

Panura   He knows all.

Pyniero   Your trap doors,
            To pop fools in at, that have no providence,

Your little wickets, to work wise men, like wire
through it;
And drag their states and bodies into Cobwebs;
Your Postern doors, to catch those that are cautious
And would not have the world's eye find their knaveries;
Your doors of danger, some men hate a pleasure,
Unless that may be full of fears; your hope doors,
And those are fine commodities, where fools pay,
For every new encouragement, a new custom;
You have your doors of honour, and of pleasure,
But those are for great Princes, glorious vanities,
That travel to be famous through diseases;
There be the doors of poverty and death too
But these you do the best you can to dam up,
For then your gain goes out.

Quisana   This is a rare lecture.

Pyniero   Read to them that understand.

Panura   Beshrew me,
I dare not venture on ye, ye cut too keen sir.

Quisana   We thank you sir for your good mirth
You are a good Companion.

Enter Quisara

Here comes the Princess now, attend your business.

Quisara   Is there no remedy? No hopes can help me?
No wit to set me free? – who's there ho?

Quisana   [*apart*]   Troubled?
Her looks are almost wild: what ails the Princess?
I know nothing she wants.

Quisara   Who's that there with you?
Oh Signior Pyniero! you are most welcome:
How does your noble uncle?

Pyniero	Sad as you are Madam:
	But he commends his service, and this Letter.

Quisara	Go off, attend within –

[Women withdraw]

Fair sir, I thank ye,
Pray be no stranger, for indeed you are welcome;
For your own virtues welcome.

Quisana	*[apart]* We are mistaken,
	This is some brave fellow sure.

Panura	*[apart]* I'm sure he's a bold fellow:
	But if she hold him so, we must believe it.

Exeunt Women

Quisara	Do you know of this fair sire?

Pyniero	I guess it Madam,
	And whither it intends: I had not brought it else.

Quisara	It is a business of no common reckoning.

Pyniero	The handsomer for him that goes about it;
	Slight actions are rewarded with slight thanks:
	Give me a matter of some weight to wade in.

Quisara	And can you love your Uncle so directly,
	So seriously, and so full, to undertake this?
	Can there be such a faith?

Pyniero	Dare you say aye to it,
	And set me on? 'tis no matter for my Uncle,
	Or what I owe to him, dare you but wish it.

Quisara	I would fain –

Pyniero	Have it done; say but so Lady.

Quisara	Conceive it so.

Pyniero   I will, 'tis that I am bound to:
Your will that must command me, and your pleasure,
The fair aspects of those eyes, that must direct me:
I am no Uncle's agent, I am mine own, Lady;
I scorn my able youth should plough for others,
Or my ambition serve for pay; I aim,
Although I never hit, as high as any man,
And the reward I reach at shall be equal,
And what love spurs me on to, this desire,
This love of you, doting upon your beauty,
The admiration of your excellence,
Makes me forget an honest man, a brave man,
A valiant, and a virtuous man, my country-man,
Armusia the delight of all, the Minion.
Make me but servant to the poorest smile,
Or the least grace you have bestow'd on others,
And see how suddenly I'll work your safety,
And set your thoughts at peace; I am no flatterer,
To promise infinitely, and out-dream dangers;
To lie abed, and swear me into Fevers,
Like some of your trim suitors; when I promise,
The light is not more constant to the world,
Than I am to my word. – [*aside*] She turns for millions.

Quisara   I have not seen a braver confirm'd courage.

Pyniero   Had I the place in your affections,
My most unworthy uncle is fit to fall from,
Liv'd in those blessed eyes, and read the stories
Of everlasting pleasures figur'd there,
I would find out your commands before you thought 'em,
And bring 'em to you done, ere you dream't of 'em.

Quisara   [*aside*] I admire his boldness.

Pyniero   This, or any thing;
Your brother's death, mine uncle's, any man's,
No state that stands secure, if you frown on it.
Look on my youth, I bring no blastings to you,
The first flower of my strength my faith –

Quisara   No more sir;
I am too willing to believe, rest satisfi'd;
If you dare do for me, I shall be thankful:
You are a handsome gentleman, a fair one,
My servant if you please; I seal it thus sir. [Kisses him]
No more, till you deserve more.

Pyniero   I am rewarded:

                                    Exit Quisara

This woman's cunning, but she's bloody too;
Although she pulls her Talons in, she's mischievous;
Form'd like the face of heaven, clear and transparent;
I must pretend still, bear 'em both in hopes,
For fear some bloody slave thrust in indeed,
Fashion'd and flesh'd to what they wish: well uncle,
What will become of this, and what dishonour
Follow this fatal shaft, if shot, let time tell,
I can but only fear, and strive to cross it.

                                              Exit

Indian women like boldness

Friends advise Armusia
to be violent with Princess

SCENE TWO

Enter Armusia, Emanuel, Soza

Emanuel Why are you thus sad? What can grieve or vex you
That have the pleasures of the world, the profits,
The honour, and the loves at your disposes?
Why should a man that wants nothing, want his quiet?

Armusia I want what beggars are above me in, content:
I want the grace I have merited, the favour,
The due respect.

Soza   Does not the King allow it?

Armusia Yes and all honours else, all I can ask,
That he has power to give; but from his sister,
The scornful cruelty, from her that should look on me,
That should a little smile upon my service,
And foster my desserts for her own faith's sake;
That should at least acknowledge me, speak to me –

Soza And you go whining up and down for this sir,
Lamenting and disputing of your grievances;
Sighing and sobbing like a sullen School-boy,
And cursing good-wife fortune for this favour?

Armusia What would you have me do?

Soza   Do what you should do,
What a man would do in this case, a wise man,
An understanding man that knows a woman;
Go to her and take her in your arms and shake her,
Take her and toss her like a bar.

Emanuel But be sure you pitch her upon a feather bed,
Shake her between a pair of sheets sir, there shake
These sullen fits out of her, spare her not there,
There you may break her will, and bruise no bone sir.

Armursia
reject suggest

Soza	Go to her.
Emanuel	That's the way.
Soza	And tell her and boldly,

And do not mince the matter.
Let her hear roundly from ye what ye are,
And what ye have deserved, and what she must be.

Emanuel   And be not put off like a common fellow
With, the Princess would be private,
Or, that she has taken physic, and admits none;
I would talk to her anywhere.

Armusia   It makes me smile.

Emanuel   Now you look handsomely:
Had I a wench to win, I would so flutter her;
They love a man that crushes 'em to verjuice;
A woman held at hard meat is your spaniel.

Soza   Pray take our counsel sir.

Armusia   I shall do something,
But not your way, it shows too boisterous,
For my affections are as fair and gentle,
As her they serve.

Enter King

Soza   The King.

King   Why, how now friend?
Why do you rob me of the company
I love so dearly sir? I have been seeking you;
For when I want you, I want all my pleasure:
Why sad? thus sad still man; I will not have it;
I must not see the face I love thus shadowed.

Emanuel   And't please your Grace, methinks it ill becomes him,
A soldier should be jovial, high and lusty.

King	He shall be so; come, come, I know your reason,
	It shall be none to cross you, ye shall have her,
	She shall be yours or nothing, pray be merry.

| Armusia | Your Grace has given me cause, I shall be sir, |
| | And ever your poor servant. |

King	Me my self sir,
	My better self. – I shall find time, and suddenly,
	To gratify your loves too gentlemen,
	Will you go with me friend?

Armusia	I beseech your grace,
	Spare me an hour or two, I shall wait on you,
	Some little private business with my self sir,
	For such a time.

King	I'll hinder no devotion;
	I'll take you gentlemen,
	Because he shall have nothing to disturb him: –
	I shall look for you friend.

| Armusia | I dare not fail sir: |

Exeunt. Manet Armusia

What shall I do to make her know my misery,
To make her sensible?

Enter Panura

This is her woman;
I have a toy come to me suddenly,
It may work for the best, she can but scorn me,
And lower than I am I cannot tumble,
I'll try what e'er my fate be. – Good even fair one.

Panura	[*aside*] 'Tis the brave stranger – A good night to you sir. –
	Now by my Lady's hand a good gentleman!
	How happy shall she be in such a husband!
	Would I were so provided too.

Armusia	Good pretty one, Shall I keep you company for an hour or two? I want employment for this evening. I am an honest man.
Panura	I dare believe ye.
Armusia	So it please you; pray let's be better acquainted, I know you are the Princess' gentlewoman, And wait upon her near.
Panura	'Tis like I do so.
Armusia	And may befriend a man, do him fair courtesies, If he have business your way.
Panura	I understand ye.
Armusia	So kind an office, that you may bind a gentleman Hereafter to be yours.
Panura	Tell me your business; Yet if it be to her, your self would do it better; The Princess must be pleas'd with your accesses, I'm sure I should.
Armusia	I want a Courtier's boldness, And am yet but a stranger, I would fain speak with her.
Panura	'Tis very late and upon her hour of sleep sir.
Armusia	Pray ye wear this, [Gives a Jewel] and believe my meaning civil, This for our more acquaintance. Kisses her
Panura	I'll do it For ten such kisses more, and 'twere high treason.
Armusia	I would be private with her.
Panura	So you shall, 'Tis not worth thanks else, you must dispatch quick.

Panura & Armusia plot (handwritten annotation)

Armusia	(Suddenly.)

Panura And I must leave you in my chamber sir,
Where you must lock your self that none may see you,
'Tis close to hers, you cannot miss the entrance,
When she comes down to bed.

Armusia I understand ye,
And once more thank ye Lady.

Panura Thank me but thus.

Kisses him

Armusia If I fail thee –

Panura Come close then.

Exeunt

SCENE THREE

Enter Quisara and Quisana

Quisara 'Tis late, good aunt, to bed, I am e'en unready,
My woman will not be long away.

Quisana I would have you a little merrier first,
Let me sit by ye, and read or discourse
Something that ye fancy, or take my instrument.

Quisara No, no I thank you,
I shall sleep without these, I wrong your age Aunt
To make ye wait thus, pray let me entreat ye,
Tomorrow I'll see ye, I know y'are sleepy,
And rest will be a welcome guest, you shall not,
Indeed you shall not stay.

Enter Panura

Oh here's my woman,
Good night, good night, and good rest Aunt attend you.

Quisana   Sleep dwell upon your eyes, and fair dreams court ye.

[Exit]

Quisara   Come, where have you been wench? Make me unready;
I slept but ill last night.

Panura   You'll sleep the better
I hope tonight Madam.

Quisara   A little rest contents me;
Thou lovest thy bed, Panura.

Panura   I am not in love Lady,
Nor seldom dream of devils, I sleep soundly.

Quisara   I'll swear thou dost, thy husband would not take it
so well
If thou wert married wench.

Panura   Let him take Madam
The way to waken me, I am no dormouse.

Quisara   Thou art a merry wench.

Panura   I shall live the longer.

Quisara   Prithee fetch my book.

Panura   I am glad of that.

Quisara   I'll read a while before I sleep.

Panura   I will Madam.

Quisara   And if Ruy Dias meet you and be importunate,
He may come in.

Panura	I have a better fare for you, Now least in sight play I.

Exit

Enter Armusia, locks the door

Quisara	Why should I love him? Why should I dote upon a man deserves not, Nor has no will to work it? who's there wench? What are you? Or whence come you?
Armusia	Ye may know me, I bring not such amazement noble Lady.
Quisara	Who let you in?
Armusia	My restless love that serves ye.
Quisara	This is an impudence I have not heard of, A rudeness that becomes a thief or ruffian; Nor shall my brother's love protect this boldness, You build so strongly on, my rooms are sanctuaries, And with that reverence they that seek my favours, And humble fears, shall render their approaches.
Armusia	Mine are no less.
Quisara	I am Mistress of my self sir, And will be so, I will not be thus visited; These fears and dangers thrust into my privacy, Stand further off, I'll cry out else.
Armusia	Oh dear Lady!
Quisara	I see dishonour in your eyes.
Armusia	There is none: By all that beauty they are innocent; Pray ye tremble not, you have no cause.

Quisara	I'll die first;

Before you have your will, be torn in pieces,
The little strength I have left me to resist you,
The gods will give me more, before I am forc'd
To that I hate, or suffer –

Armusia	You wrong my duty.

Quisara   So base a violation of my liberty?
I know you are bent unnobly; I'll take to me
The spirit of a man, borrow his boldness,
And force my woman's fears into a madness,
And ere you arrive at what you aim at –

Armusia   Lady,
If there be in you any woman's pity,   [*Kneels*]
And if your fears have not proclaim'd me monstrous,
Look on me and believe me; is this violence?
Is it to fall thus prostrate to your beauty
A ruffian's boldness? Is humility a rudeness?
The griefs and sorrows that grow here an impudence?
And thus high has your brother's favour blown me:
Alas dear Lady of my life, I came not
With any purpose rough, or desperate,
With any thought that was not smooth and gentle
As your fair hand,
Far be it from my heart to fright your quiet.

Quisara   Now I dare hear you.

Armusia   If you misdoubt still,
                        [*Rises, offers his sword*]
Take this and sheath it here; be your own safety;
Be wise, and rid your fears, and let me perish;
How willing shall I sleep to satisfy you.

Quisara   No, I believe now, you speak worthily;
What came you then for?

Armusia	To complain me, beauty,

But modestly.

Quisara	Of what?

Armusia	Of your fierce cruelty;

Humbly to tell your grace, ye had forgot me:
Pray pardon me that I use this liberty
To show what I have done to deserve ye;
To tell ye, and by my life ye may believe me,
That I am honest, and will only marry
You, or your memory; pray not be angry.

Quisara   I thank you sir, and let me tell you seriously,
Ye have taken now the right way to befriend ye,
And to beget a fair and clear opinion,
Yet to try your obedience –

Armusia	I stand ready Lady.

Quisara   Without presuming to ask any thing,
Or at this time to hope for further favour;
Or to remember services, or smiles;
Dangers you have pass'd through, and rewards due to 'em;
Loves or despairs but leaving all to me:
Quit this place presently.

Armusia	I shall obey ye.

Enter Ruy Dias

Ruy Dias	Ha?

Armusia	Who's this? What art thou?

Ruy Dias	A Gentleman.

Armusia   Thou art no more I'm sure: – [*aside*] oh 'tis Ruy Dias;
How high he looks, and harsh!

Princess changes her mind about Dias and Armusia

Ruy Dias	Is there not door enough, You take such elbow room?
Armusia	If I take it, I'll carry it.
Ruy Dias	Does this become you Princess?
Armusia	The Captain's jealous, Jealous of that he never durst deserve yet; Go freely, go I'll give thee leave.
Ruy Dias	Your leave sir?
Armusia	Yes my leave sir, I'll not be troubled neither, Nor shall my heart ache, or my head be jealous, Nor strange suspicious thought reign in my memory; Go on, and do thy worst, I'll smile at thee; – I kiss your fair hand first, – then farewell Captain.

                                                                        [*Exit*]

Quisara	[*aside*] What a pure soul inherits here! What innocence! Sure I was blind when I first lov'd this fellow, And long'd to live in that fog still: how he blusters!
Ruy Dias	Am I your property? or those your flatteries, The banquets that ye bid me to, the trust I build my goodly hopes on?
Quisara	Be more temperate.
Ruy Dias	Are these the shows of your respect and favour? What did he here? What language had he with ye? Did ye invite him? Could ye stay no longer? Is he gracious in your eye?
Quisara	You are too forward.
Ruy Dias	Why at these private hours?

Marriage

Dias is harsh – brute   Indian
Armusia is pure – civilized

Quisara   You are too saucy,
                    Too impudent to task me with those errors:
                    Do ye know what I am sir, and my prerogative?
                    Though you be a thing I have call'd by th' name of friend,
                    I never taught you to dispose my liberty;
                    How durst you touch mine honour? Blot my meanings?
                    And name an action, and of mine but noble?
                    Thou poor unworthy thing, how have I grac'd thee?
                    How have I nourish'd thee, and raised thee hourly?
                    Are these the gratitudes you bring, Ruy Dias?
                    The thanks? The services? I am fairly paid;
                    Was't not enough I saw thou wert a Coward,
                    And shadowed thee? No noble sparkle in thee?
                    Daily provok'd thee and still found thee coward?
                    Rais'd noble causes for thee, strangers started at;
                    Yet still, still, still a Coward, ever Coward;
                    And with those taints, dost thou upbraid my virtues?

Ruy Dias   I was to blame, Lady.

Quisara   So blindly bold to touch at my behaviour?
                    If thou hadst been a brave fellow, thou hadst had some
                                                                        licence,
                    Some liberty I might have then allowed thee;
                    But being nothing but a sound, a shape,
                    The mere sign of a Soldier – of a Lover
                    The dregs and draffy part, disgrace and jealousy,
                    I scorn thee, and condemn thee.

Ruy Dias   Dearest Lady,
                    If I have been too free –

Quisara   Thou hast been too foolish,
                    And go on still; I'll study to forget thee, –
                    I would I could – and yet I pity thee.

                                                                    Exit

Ruy Dias   I am not worth it; if I were, that's misery,
            The next door is but death, I must aim at it.

                                                          Exit

Dias is sorry(?)

Gov disguised as a monk tries to discredit Portugals.

ACT FOUR

SCENE ONE

Enter King and Governor like a Moor Priest

King   So far and truly you have discovered to me
              The former currents of my life and fortune,
              That I am bound to acknowledge ye most holy,
              And certainly to credit your prediction
              Of what are yet to come.

Governor   I am no liar. –

King   Pray ye sit good father,
              Certain a reverend man, and most religious.

Governor   Aye, that belief's well now, and let me work then.
              I'll make ye curse religion ere I leave ye: –
              I have liv'd a long time son, a mew'd up man,
              Sequester'd by the special hand of heaven
              From the world's vanities, bid farewell to follies,
              And shook hands with all heats of youth and pleasures;
              As in a dream these twenty years I have slumber'd,
              Many a cold moon have I in meditation,
              Lain shaking under, many a burning Sun
              Has sear'd my body, and boil'd up my blood,
              Feebled my knees, and stamp'd a Meagerness
              Upon my figure, all to find out knowledge,
              Which I have now attained too, thanks to heaven,
              All for my country's good too, and many a vision,
              Many a mystic vision have I seen son,
              And many a sight from heaven which has been terrible,

Wherein the goods and evils of these Islands
Were lively shadowed; now I am come son,
The hour is now appointed, my tongue is touch'd,
And now I speak.

King   Do holy man, I'll hear ye.

Governor   Beware these Portugals, I say beware 'em,
These smooth fac'd strangers, have an eye upon 'em.
The cause is now the Gods, hear, and believe King.

King   I do hear, but before I give rash credit,
Know I have found 'em gentle, faithful, valiant,
And am bound to 'em for my deliverance.

Governor   O Son, the future aims of men, observe me,
Above their present actions, and their glory,
Are to be look'd at: the stars show many turnings,
If you could see, mark but with my eye's pupil:
These men came hither as my vision tells me,
Poor, weatherbeaten, almost lost, starv'd, feebled,
Their vessels like themselves, most miserable;
Made a long suit for traffic, and for comfort,
To vent their children's toys, cure their diseases:
They had their suit, they landed and to th'rate
Grew rich and powerful, suck'd the fat, and freedom
Of this most blessed Isle, taught her to tremble;
Witness the Castle here, the Citadel,
They have clapp'd upon the neck of your Tidore,
This happy town, till that she knew these strangers,
To check her when she's jolly.

King   They have so indeed father.

Governor   Take heed, take heed, I find your fair delivery,
Though you be pleas'd to glorify that fortune,
And think these strangers Gods, take heed I say,
I find it but a handsome preparation,

A fair fac'd Prologue to a further mischief:
Mark but the end good King, the pin he shoots at
That was the man deliver'd ye; the mirror,
Your Sister is his due; what's she, your heir sir?
And what's he akin then to? the Kingdom.
But heirs are not ambitious, who then suffers?
What reverence shall the Gods have? And what justice
The miserable people? What shall they do?

King   [*aside*] He points at truth directly.

Governor   Think of these son:
The person, nor the manner I mislike not
Of your preserver, nor the whole man together,
Were he but season'd in the faith we are,
In our devotions learn'd.

King   You say right father.

Governor   To change our worships now, and our Religion?
To be traitor to our Gods?

King   You have well advised me,
And I will seriously consider father;
In the meantime you shall have your fair access
Unto my sister, advise her to your purpose,
And let me still know how the Gods determine.

Governor   I will – [*aside*] But my main end is to advise
The destruction of you all, a general ruin,
And then I am reveng'd; let the Gods whistle.

                   Exeunt

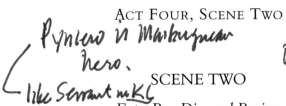

Pyniero is Marbuzcan hero.

— like Servant makc

Dias changes his tune

SCENE TWO

Enter Ruy Dias and Pyniero

Ruy Dias   Indeed, I am right glad ye were not greedy,
And sudden in performing what I will'd you,
Upon the person of Armusia;
I was afraid, for I well knew your valour,
And love to me.

Pyniero   'Twas not a fair thing uncle,
It show'd not handsome, carried no man in it.

Ruy Dias   I must confess 'twas ill, and I abhor it,
Only this good has risen from this evil;
I have tried your honesty, and find it proof,
A constancy that will not be corrupted,
And I much honour it.

Pyniero   This Bell sounds better.

Ruy Dias   My anger now, and that disgrace I have suffer'd,
Shall be more manly vented, and wip'd off,
And my sick honour cur'd the right and straight way;
My Sword's in my hand now nephew, my cause upon it,
And man to man, one valour to another,
My hope to his.

Pyniero   Why! This is like Ruy Dias!
This carries something of some substance in it;
To kill men scurvily, 'tis such a dog trick,
Such a rat-catcher's occupation –

Ruy Dias   It is no better,
But Pyniero now –

Pyniero   Now you do bravely.

Ruy Dias	The difference of our states flung by, forgotten,
	The full opinion I have won in service,
	Laid handsomely aside, only our fortunes,
	And single manhoods –
Pyniero	In a service sir,
	Of this most noble nature, all I am,
	If I had ten lives more, those and my fortunes
	Are ready for ye; I had thought ye had
	Forsworn fighting, or banish'd those brave thoughts
	Were wont to wait upon you; I am glad
	To see 'em call'd home again.
Ruy Dias	They are nephew,
	And thou shalt see what fire they carry in them;
	Shows a Challenge
	Here, you guess what this means.
Pyniero	Yes, very well sir.
Ruy Dias	As soon as you can find him –
Pyniero	That will not be long uncle,
	And o' my conscience he'll be ready as quickly.
Ruy Dias	I make no doubt good Nephew, carry it so
	If you can possible that we may fight –
Pyniero	Nay, you shall fight assure your self.
Ruy Dias	Pray ye hear me,
	In some such place where it may be possible
	The Princess may behold us.
Pyniero	I conceive ye,
	Upon the sand behind the Castle sir,
	A place remote enough, and there be windows
	Out of her lodgings too, or I am mistaken.

Ruy Dias	Y'are i'th' right, if ye can work that handsomely +
Pyniero	Let me alone, and pray you be prepar'd Some three hours hence.
Ruy Dias	I will not fail.
Pyniero	Get you home, And if you have any things to dispose of, or a few light prayers That may befriend you, run 'em over quickly, I warrant, I'll bring him on.
Ruy Dias	Farewell Nephew, And when we meet again –
Pyniero	Aye, aye, fight handsomely;

[Exit Ruy Dias]

Take a good draught or two of wine to settle ye,
'Tis an excellent armour for an ill conscience Uncle;–
I am glad to see this man's conversion,
I was afraid fair honour had been bedrid,
Or beaten out o'th' Island. He will fight now;
And, I believe too, bravely; I have seen him
Curry a fellow's carcass handsomely:
And in the head of a troop stand as if he had been
rooted there,
Dealing large doles of death; what a rascal was I
I did not see his will drawn!

[Enter Quisara]

[aside]   What does she here?
Now what new business is for me?

Quisara	I was sending for ye, But since we have met so fair, you have sav'd that labour; I must entreat you sir –

Pyniero   Any thing Madam,
                    Your wills are my commands.

Quisara   Y'are nobly courteous;
                    Upon my better thoughts Signior Pyniero,
                    I would desire you to attempt no farther
                    Against the person of the noble stranger,
                    Nor be incited further by your uncle,
                    Good sir desist –

Pyniero   You speak now like a woman,
tenderness   And wondrous well this tenderness becomes ye;
                    But this you must remember – your command
                    Was laid on with a kiss, and seriously
                    It must be taken off the same way Madam,
                    Or I stand bound still.

Quisara   That shall not endanger ye,
                    Look ye fair sir, thus I take off that duty.

                                                    [*Kisses him*]

Pyniero   By th' mass 'twas soft and sweet; some bloods would
                                                        bound now,
                    And run a tilt; do not you think bright beauty,
Chivalry   You have done me in the kiss a mighty favour,
                    And that I stand bound by virtue of this honour,
                    To do whatever you command me?

Quisara   I think sir,
                    From me these are unusual courtesies,
                    And ought to be respected so; there are some,
                    And men of no mean rank, would hold themselves
                    Not poorly bless'd to taste of such a bounty.

Pyniero   I know there are that would do many unjust things
                    For such a provocation, kill their kindred,
                    Demolish the fair credits of their Parents;

Those kisses I am not acquainted with;
'Tis the devil's own dance, to be kiss'd into cruelty.

Quisara   I am glad you make that use sir.

Pyniero   I am gladder
That you made me believe you were cruel,
For by this hand I know I am so honest,
I would not kill a dog for a woman;
She must be a good woman made me kick him,
And that will be hard to find: To kill a man…

Quisara   I take it in you well.

Pyniero   I thank ye Lady,
And I shall study to confirm it.

Quisara   Do sir,
For this time, and this present cause I 'llow it.

                                    [Exit Pyniero]

        Enter Governor disguised, Quisana and Panura

Governor   Bless ye my royal daughter,
And in you, bless this Island heaven.

Quisara   Good Aunt,
What think ye of this man?

Quisana   Sure 'is a wise man,
And a religious; he tells us things have happened
So many years ago almost forgotten,
As readily, as if they were done this hour.

Quisana   [to Panura] Does he not meet with your sharp tongue?

Panura   He tells me Madam,
Marriage and mouldy cheese will make me tamer.

gov, as priest, convinces Princess against Portugals

Governor	A stubborn keeper, and worse fare,
	An open stable and cold care,
	Will tame a Jade, may be your share.
Panura	By'r Lady, a sharp prophet; when this proves good
	I'll bequeath you a skin to make ye a hood.
Governor	Lady I would talk with you.
Quisara	Do reverend sir.
Governor	And give ear wisely to me.
Quisara	I shall father.
Governor	You are a Princess of that excellence,
	Sweetness and grace, that Angel-like fair feature –
	Nay do not blush, I do not flatter you,
	Nor do I dote in telling this – I am amaz'd Lady;
	And, as I think, the gods bestow'd these on ye,
	The gods that love ye.
Quisara	I confess their bounty.
Governor	Apply it then to their use, to their honour,
	They have an instant great use of your goodness;
	The Portugals like sharp thorns (mark me Lady)
	Stick in our sides; like razors, wound religion,
	Draw deep, they wound, till the life blood follows,
	Our gods they spurn at, and their worships scorn,
	A mighty hand they bear upon our government.
	These are the men your miracle must work on,
	Your heavenly form, either to root them out,
	To nip their memory, that may not spring more,
	Or fairly bring 'em home to our devotions,
	Which will be blessed, and for which, you sainted: –
	[*aside*] But cannot be; and they go, let me buzzle.
Quisara	Go up with me, where we'll converse more privately;

I'll show ye shortly how I hold their temper;
And in what chain their souls.

Governor   Keep fast that hold still,
And either bring that chain, and those bound in it,
And link it to our gods, and their fair worships,
Or daughter pinch their hearts a-pieces with it;
I'll wait upon your grace.

Quisara   Come reverend father. –
Wait you below.

                              [*Exeunt Quisara and Governor*]

Panura   If this prophet were a young thing,
I should suspect him now, he cleaves so close to her;
These holy coats are long, and hide iniquities.

Quisana   Away, away fool, a poor wretch.

Panura   These poor ones,
Warm but their stomachs once –

Quisana   Come in, thou art foolish.

                                               Exeunt

SCENE THREE

Enter Armusia, Emanuel, Pyniero

Armusia   I am sorry sir my fortune is so stubborn,
To court my sword against my countryman,
Your person, nor your uncle's am I angry with,
And I protest, I had rather use my sword
In your defences, than against your safeties;
'Tis methinks, a strange dearth of enemies,
When we seek foes amongst our selves.

Emanuel   You are injured,
And you must take the best on't now, and readiest –

Armusia   You see I am ready in the place, and arm'd
To his desire that call'd me.

Pyniero   Ye speak honestly,
And I could wish ye had met on terms more friendly,
But it cannot now be so.

Enter Ruy Dias

Emanuel   Turn sir, and see.

Pyniero   I have kept my word with ye uncle,
The Gentleman is ready.

Enter Governor disguised, and Quisara above

Armusia   [*to Ruy Dias*]   Ye are welcome.

Ruy Dias   Bid those fools welcome that affect your courtesy,
I come not to use compliment; ye have wrong'd me,
And ye shall feel proud man ere I part from ye,
The effects of that, if fortune do not fool me;
Thy life is mine, and no hope shall redeem thee.

Armusia   That's a proud word, more than your faith can justify.

Quisara   [*apart*] Sure they will fight.

Ruy Dias   [*aside*]   She's there, I am happy.

Governor   [*apart*] Let 'em alone, let 'em kill one another: –
[*aside*] These are the main posts, if they fall, the buildings
Will tumple quickly.

Quisara   [*apart*]   How temperate Armusia!

Governor   [*apart*] No more, be quiet yet.

Armusia	I am not bloody,

Nor do not feel such mortal malice in me,
But since we cannot both enjoy the Princess,
I am resolv'd to fight.

Ruy Dias   Fight home Armusia,
For if thou faint'st, or fall'st –

Armusia   Do ye make all vantages?

Ruy Dias   Stand still I charge ye nephew, as ye honour me.

Armusia   And good Emanuel stir not –

Pyniero   Ye speak fitly,
For we had not stood idle else.

Governor   [*aside*]   I am sorry for't.

Emanuel   But since you will have it so –

Ruy Dias   Come sir.

Armusia   I wait ye

                                        [*They fight*]

Pyniero   I marry this looks handsomely, this is warm work.

Governor   [*aside*] Both fall an't be thy will.

                                        Ruy Dias falls

Pyniero   My Uncle dead?

Emanuel   Stand still, or my sword's in –

Armusia   Now, brave Ruy Dias,
Now where's your confidence? Your prayers, quickly:
Your own spirit has condemn'd ye.

Quisara   Hold, Armusia.

Armusia	Most happy Lady.

Quisara   Hold and let him rise,
Spare him for me.

Armusia   A long and happy life may he enjoy Lady.

Governor   What ha' you done? 'tis better they had all perish'd.

Quisara   Peace father, I work for the best; – Armusia,
Be in the garden an hour hence.

Armusia   I shall Madam.

Exeunt Quisara and Governor

Why are ye sad sir? How would this have griev'd you,
If ye had fall'n under a profess'd enemy?
Under one had taken vantage of your shame too?
Pray ye be at peace, I am so far from wronging ye,
Or glorying in the pride of such a victory,
That I desire to serve ye, pray look cheerfully.

Pyniero   Do you hear this sir? Why do you hold your head down?
Come, come, thank fortune and your friend.

Ruy Dias   Sir you have beat me both ways, yet so nobly,
That I shall ever love the hand that did it:
Fortune make me worthy of some title
That may be near your friend.

Armusia   Sir I must leave ye,
But with so hearty love, and pray be confident,
I carry nothing from this place shall wrong ye.

Exeunt Armusia and Emanuel

Pyniero   Come, come, you are right again, sir, love your honour,
And love your friend, make your fame your mistress,
And let these trinkets go.

Dias/armosia freinds

Ruy Dias   You teach well nephew,
Now to be honourable even with this Gentleman,
Shall be my business, and my ends his.

                                                        Exeunt

                          SCENE FOUR   *now as priest
                                            & King*

                Enter Governor disguised and King

Governor   Sir, sir, you must do something suddenly,
To stop his pride, so great and high he is shot up,
Upon his person too, your state is sunk else:
You must not stand now upon terms of gratitude,
And let a simple tenderness besot ye:
I'll bring ye suddenly where you shall see him,
Attempting your brave sister privately,
Mark but his high behaviour then.

King   I will Father.

Governor   And with scorn, I fear, contempt too.

King   I hope not.

Governor   I will not name a lust; it may be that also;
A little force must be applied upon him,
Now, now applied, a little force to humble him.
These sweet entreaties do but make him wanton.

King   Take heed ye wrong him not.

Governor   Take heed to your safety,
I but forewarn ye King; if you mistrust me,
Or think I come unsent –

King   No, I'll go with you.

                                                        Exeunt

Princess give up his faith (handwritten annotation)

cp with F&M. (handwritten annotation)

SCENE FIVE

Enter Armusia, Quisara

courtly love seems quaint to other character (handwritten annotation)

Armusia   Madam, you see there's nothing I can reach at,
            Either in my obedience, or my service,
            That may deserve your love, or win a liking,
            Not a poor thought, but I pursue it seriously,
            Take pleasure in your wills, even in your anger,
            Which other men would grudge at, and grow stormy;
            Pray Madam but consider –

Quisara   Yes I do sir,
            And to that honest end I drew ye hither;
            I know ye have deserv'd as much as man can,
            And know it is a justice to requite you:
            I know ye love.

Armusia   If ever love was mortal,
            And dwelt in man; and for that love command me
            Do something of such a greatness
            Those things I have done already, may seem foils to.

Iago Duke in M&M (handwritten annotation)

Enter Governor disguised, and King and stand apart

Governor   [apart]
            Now stand close King and hear, and as you find him,
            Believe me right, or let religion suffer.

Quisara   I dare believe your worth without additions;
            But since you are so liberal of your love sir,
            And would be farther tried, I do intend it,
            Because you shall not, or you would not win me
            At such an easy rate.

Armusia   I am prepared still,
            And if I shrink –

Quisara	I know ye are no coward,
	This is the utmost trial of your constancy,
	And if you stand fast now, I am yours, your wife sir;
	You hold there is nothing dear that may achieve me,
	Doubted or dangerous.
Armusia	There's nothing, nothing:
	Let me but know, that I may straight fly to it.
Quisara	I'll tell you then: change your religion,
	And be of one belief with me.
Armusia	How?
Quisara	Mark,
	Worship our Gods, renounce that faith you are bred in;
	'Tis easily done, I'll teach ye suddenly;
	And humbly on your knees –
Armusia	Ha? I'll be hang'd first.
Quisara	Offer as we do.
Armusia	To the Devil, Lady?
	Offer to him I hate? I know the devil;
	To dogs and cats? You make offer to them;
	To every bird that flies, and every worm.
	How terribly I shake! Is this the venture?
	The trial that you talk'd of? where have I been?
	And how forgot my self? how lost my memory?
	When did I pray or look up steadfastly?
	Had any goodness in my heart to guide me?
	That I should give this vantage to mine enemy,
	The enemy to my peace; forsake my faith?
Quisara	Come, come, I know ye love me.
Armusia	Love ye this way?
	This most destroying way? Sure you but jest Lady.

Quisara	My love and life are one way.

Armusia   And mine another way;
Love alone then, I'll love diseases first;
Dote on a villain that would cut my throat,
Woo all afflictions of all sorts, kiss cruelty;
Have mercy heaven, how have I been wand'ring?
Wand'ring the way of lust, and left my maker?
How have I slept like a Cork upon a water,
And had no feeling of the storm that toss'd me?
Trod the blind paths of death? Forsook assurance,
Eternity of blessedness for a woman?
For a young handsome face hazard my being?

Quisara   Are not our powers eternal? So their comforts
As great and full of hopes as yours?

Armusia   They are puppets.

Governor   [*aside*] Now mark him sir, and but observe him nearly.

Armusia   Their comforts like themselves, cold senseless outsides;
You make 'em sick, as we are, peevish, mad,
Subject to age; and how can they cure us,
That are not able to refine themselves?

Quisara   The Sun and Moon we worship, those are heavenly,
And their bright influences we believe.

Armusia   Away fool,
I adore the Maker of that Sun and Moon,
That gives those bodies light and influence,
Shall I fall from this faith to please a woman?
For her embraces bring my soul to ruin?
I look'd you should have said, make me a Christian,
Work that great cure, for 'tis a great one woman;
That labour truly do perform, that venture
The crown of all great trial, and the fairest:
I look'd ye should have wept and kneel'd to beg it,

Wash'd off your mist of ignorance, with waters
Pure and repentant, from those eyes; I look'd
You should have brought me your chief god ye worship,
He that you offer human blood and life to,
And made a sacrifice of him to memory,
Beat down his Altars, ruin'd his false Temples.

Governor   [apart] Now you may see.

Quisara   Take heed, you go too far sir, –
                lasvivia
             [aside] And yet I love to hear him; – I must have ye,
             (And to that end I let you storm a little);
             Have ye of my faith too, and so enjoy ye.

Armusia   How I condemn ye, and I hate my self
             For looking on that face lasciviously,
             And it looks ugly now methinks.

Quisara   How, Portugal?

Armusia   It looks like death it self, to which 'twould lead me;
             Your eyes resemble pale despair, they fright me,
             And in their rounds a thousand horrid ruins,
             Methinks I see; and in your tongue hear fearfully
             The hideous murmurs weak souls have suffer'd;
             Get from me, I despise ye, and know woman,
             That for all this trap you have laid to catch my life in,
             To catch my immortal life, I hate and curse ye,
             Condemn your deities, spurn at their powers,
             And where I meet your maumet Gods, I'll swing 'em
             Thus o'er my head, and kick 'em into puddles,
             Nay I will out of vengeance search your Temples,
             And with those hearts that serve my God, demolish
             Your shambles of wild worships.

Governor   [apart]   Now, now you hear sir.

Armusia   I will have my faith since you are so crafty,
             The glorious cross; although I love your brother,

Let him frown too, I will have my devotion,
And let your whole State storm.

King   [*to Guards within*]   Enter and take him: –

                [*Enter Guards and bind Armusia*]

                I am sorry friend that I am forc'd to do this.

Governor   Be sure you bind him fast.

Quisara   But use him nobly.

King   Had it to me been done, I had forgiven it,
                And still preserv'd you fair, but to our Gods sir –

Quisara   [*aside*] Methinks I hate 'em now.

King   To our Religion,
                To these to be thus stubborn, thus rebellious
                To threaten them.

Armusia   Use all your violence,
                I ask no mercy, nor repent my words;
                I spit at your best powers; I serve one,
                Will give me strength to scourge your gods –

Governor   Away with him.

Armusia   To grind 'em into base dust, and disperse 'em,
                That never more their bloody memories –

Governor   Clap him close up.

King   Good friend be cooler.

Armusia   Never;
                Your painted sister I despise too.

King   Softly.

Armusia   And all her devilish arts laugh and scorn at,
Mock her blind purposes.

King   You must be temperate; –
Offer him no violence I command you strictly.

                                         Exeunt Guards with Armusia

Governor   [*aside*] Now thou art up I shall have time to speak too.

Quisara   [*aside*] Oh how I love this man, how truly honour him.

                                                       Exeunt

ACT FIVE

SCENE ONE

Enter Christophero, and Pedro (at one door),
Emanuel and Soza (at another)

Christophero Do you know the news Gentlemen?

Emanuel Would we knew as well sir
How to prevent it.

Soza Is this the love they bear us
For our late benefit? taken so maliciously,
And clapp'd up close? is that the thanks they render?

Christophero It must not be put up thus, smother'd sleightly,
'Tis such a base unnatural wrong.

Pedro I know,
They may think to do wonders, aim at all,
And to blow us with a vengeance out o'th'Islands:
But if we be our selves, honest and resolute,
And continue but Masters of our ancient courages,
Stick close and give no vantage to their villainies –

Soza Nay if we faint or fall a-pieces now,
We are fools and worthy to be mark'd for misery;
Begin to strike at him they are all bound to?
To cancel his desserts? What must we look for
If they can carry this?

Emanuel I'll carry coals then;
I have but one life, and one fortune Gentlemen,

But I'll so husband it to vex these rascals,
These barbarous slaves.

Christophero   Shall we go charge 'em presently?

Soza   No that will be too weak, and too foolhardy,
We must have grounds that promise safety friends,
And sure offence; we lose our angers else,
And worse than that, venture our lives too lightly.

Enter Pyniero

Pyniero   Did you see mine Uncle? Plague 'a these Barbarians,
How the rogues stick in my teeth; I know ye are angry,
So I am too, monstrous angry Gentlemen,
I am angry that I choke again.
You hear Armusia's up, honest Armusia,
Clapp'd up in prison friends, the brave Armusia,
Here are fine boys.

Emanuel   We hope he shall not stay there.

Pyniero   Stay? No he must not stay, no talk of staying,
These are not times to stay; are not these Rascals?
Speak, I beseech ye speak, are they not Rogues?
Think some abominable names – are they not Devils?
But the devil's a great deal too good for 'em – fusty villains.

Christophero They are a kind of hounds.

Pyniero   Hounds were their fathers,
Old blear-eyed bob-tail'd hounds – Lord where's
                                        my Uncle?

Soza   But what shall be done sir?

Pyniero   Done?

Soza   Yes to relieve him;
If it be not sudden they may take his life too.

Pyniero	They dare as soon take fire and swallow it,
	Take stakes and thrust into their tails for glisters:
	His life? Why 'tis a thing worth all the Islands,
	His very imprisonment will make the Town stink,
	And shake and stink, I have physic in my hand for 'em
	Shall give the goblins such a purge –

Enter Ruy Dias

Pedro	Your Uncle.
Ruy Dias	I hear strange news, and have been seeking ye;
	They say Armusia's prisoner.
Pyniero	'Tis most certain.
Ruy Dias	Upon what cause?
Pyniero	He has deserv'd too much sir;
	You are the next if you can carry it tamely;
	He has deserved of all.
Ruy Dias	I must confess it,
	Of me so nobly too.
Pyniero	I am glad to hear it,
	You have a time now to make good your confession,
	Now to redeem all. You are a Gentleman,
	And honest man, and you dare love your Nation,
	Dare stick to virtue though she be oppress'd,
	And for her own fair sake step to her Rescue:
	If you live ages sir, and lose this hour,
	Your life will be a murmur, and no man in't.
Ruy Dias	I thank ye nephew, – come along with me Gentlemen,
	We'll make 'em dancing sport immediately:
	We are Masters of the Fort yet, we shall see
	What that can do.
Pyniero	Let it but spit fire finely,
	And play their turrets and their painted Palaces

A frisking round or two, that they may trip it,
And caper in the air.

Ruy Dias   Come, we'll do something
Shall make 'em look about, we'll send 'em plums
Too hard for their teeth.

Pyniero   And fine Potatoes
Roasted in gunpowder,

Ruy Dias   They shall see
There is no safe retreat in villainy;
Come be high hearted all.

Omnes   We are all on fire sir.

                    Exeunt

                    SCENE TWO

Enter King and Governor disguised, and Guard

King   I am ungrateful, and a wretch, persuade me not;
Forgetful of the mercy he show'd me,
The timely noble pity – Why should I
See him fast bound whose mighty hand set me free?

Governor   Had the offence been thrown on you, 'tis certain
It had been in your power to have turn'd it into mercy,
But since the cause concerns the honour of our gods,
And so transcends your power, and your compassion,
A little your own safety if you saw it too,
If your too fond indulgence did not dazzle you,
It cannot now admit a private pity;
'Tis in their wills, their mercies, or revenges,
And these revolts in you show mere rebellious.

King	They are mild and pitiful.
Governor	To those repent.
King	Their nature's soft and tender.

Governor   To true hearts
That feel compunction for their trespasses:
This man defies 'em still, threatens destruction
And demolition of their arms and worship,
Spits at their powers;

King   What shall I do
To deserve of this man –

Governor   If ye more bemoan him,
Or mitigate your power to preserve him,
I'll curse ye from the gods, call up their vengeance.
And fling it on your Land and you, I have charge for't: –
[*aside*] I hope to wrack you all.

Enter Quisara with her hands bound, Quisana, Panura

King   What ails my sister?
Why is she bound? Why looks she so distractedly?
Who dares do this?

Quisana   We did it, pardon sir,
And for her preservation – She is grown wild,
And raving on the stranger's love and honour,
Sometimes crying out, 'Help, help, they will torture him,
They will take his life, they will murder him':presently,
If we had not prevented, violently,
Had laid hands on her own life.

Governor   These are tokens
The gods' displeasure is gone out; be quick,
And ere it fall do something to appease 'em,
You know the sacrifice: – [*aside*] I am glad it works thus.

Quisara   How low and base thou lookst now that wert noble.
           No figure of a King methinks shows on you,
           No face of Majesty; foul swarth ingratitude
           Has taken off thy sweetness, base forgetfulness
           Of mighty benefits, has turned thee Devil:
           Thou has wrong'd thine own preserver,
           What hast thou done?

Governor   Go for him presently: –

                                             [*Exeunt Guard*]

           Do you know what you say Lady?

Quisara   I could curse thee too,
           Religion and severity has steel'd thee,
           Has turn'd thy heart to stone?
           None of ye feel what bravery ye tread on?
           What innocence? What beauty?

King   Pray be patient.

Quisara   What honourable things ye cast behind ye?
           What monuments of man?

                  Enter Armusia and Guard

King   Once more Armusia,
           Because I love ye tenderly and dearly,
           Even from my heart I wish and woo ye –

Armusia   What sir?
           Take heed how ye persuade me falsely, then ye hate me;
           Take heed how ye entrap me.

King   I advise ye,
           And tenderly and truly I advise ye,
           Both for your soul's health and your safety –

Armusia   Stay,
           And name my soul no more, – touch my life,

Torture

martyr

'Tis ready for ye, put it to what test
It shall please ye, I am patient; but for the rest
You may remove rocks with your little fingers,
Or blow a mountain out o'th'way, with bellows,
As soon as stir my faith, use no more arguments.

Governor   We must use tortures then.

Armusia   Your worst and painfull'st
I am joyful to accept.

Governor   You must the sharpest,
For such has been your hate against our deities
Delivered openly, your threats and scornings;
And either your repentance must be mighty,
Which is your free conversion to our customs,
Or equal punishment, which is your life sir.

Armusia   I am glad I have it for ye, take it Priest,
And all the miseries that shall attend it;
Let the Gods glut themselves with Christian blood:
Your Gods of gold shall melt and sink before it;
Your Altars, and your Temples shake to nothing;
And you false worshippers, blind fools of ceremony,
Shall seek for holes to hide your heads, and fears in,
For seas to swallow you from this destruction,
Darkness to dwell about ye, and conceal ye,
Your mothers' wombs again –

Governor   Make the fires ready,
And bring the several tortures out.

[Exit one of the Guard]

Quisara   Stand fast sir,
And fear 'em not; you that have stepp'd so nobly
Into this pious trial, start not now,
Keep on your way, a virgin will assist ye,
A virgin won by your fair constancy,

And glorying that she is won so, will die by ye;
I have touch'd ye every way, tried ye most honest,
Perfect, and good, chaste, blushing-chaste, and temperate,
Indeed, the perfect school of worth I find ye,
The temple of true honour.

Armusia   [*aside*]   Whither will she? –
What do you infer by this fair argument Lady?

Quisara   I do embrace your faith sir, and your fortune;
Go on, I will assist ye, I feel a sparkle here,
A lively spark that kindles my affection,
And tells me it will rise to flames of glory:
Let 'em put on their angers, suffer nobly,
Show me the way, and when I faint instruct me;
And if I follow not –

Armusia   O blessed Lady,

                                              [*Embraces her*]

Since thou art won, let me begin my triumph, –
Come clap your terrors on.

Quisara   All your fell tortures.
For there is nothing he shall suffer brother,
I swear by my new faith which is most sacred,
And I will keep it so, but I will follow in,
And follow to a scruple of affliction,
In spite of all your Gods.

Governor   [*aside*]   Death, she amazes me.

King   What shall be done now?

Governor   They must die both,
And suddenly; they will corrupt all else; –
[*aside*] This woman makes me weary of my mischief,
She shakes me, and she staggers me: – go in sir,
I'll see the execution.

King   Not so sudden;
            If they go all my friends and sisters perish.

Governor   [aside] Would I were safe at home again.

                        Enter Syana

Syana   Arm, arm sir,
            Seek for defence, the Castle plays and thunders,
            The Town Rocks, and the houses fly i'th' air,
            The people die for fear – Captain Ruy Dias,
            Has made an Oath he will not leave a stone here,
            No not the memory, here has stood a City,
            Unless Armusia be deliver'd fairly.

King   I have my fears: what can our gods do now for us?

Governor   Be patient, but keep him still: he is a cure sir
            Against both rage and Cannon: go and fortify,
            Call in the Princes, make the Palace sure,
            And let 'em know you are a King: look nobly;
            And take your courage to ye; keep close the prisoner,
            And under command, we are betray'd else.

Armusia   How joyfully I go!

Quisara   Take my heart with thee.

Governor   [aside] I hold a Wolf by the ear now: Fortune free me.

                                            Exeunt

                        SCENE THREE
                    [*Omitted from this production*]

SCENE FOUR

Enter Pyniero and Panura

Pyniero Art sure it was that blind priest?

Panura   Yes most certain,
He has provok'd all this; the King is merciful,
And wondrous loving; but he fires him on still,
And when he cools enrages him, I know it;
Threatens new vengeance, and the gods' fierce justice
When he but looks with fair eyes on Armusia;
Will lend him no time to relent; my royal Mistress,
She has entertain'd a Christian hope.

Pyniero   Speak truly.

Panura Nay 'tis most true,
And I fear, if not speedily prevented,
If she continue stout, both shall be executed.

Pyniero I'll kiss thee for this news: nay more Panura,
If thou wilt give me leave, I'll get thee with Christian,
The best way to convert thee.

Panura   Make me believe so.

Pyniero I will i'faith. But which way cam'st thou hither?
The Palace is close guarded, and barricado'd.

Panura I came through a private vault, which few there know of;
It rises in a Temple not far hence,
Close by the Castle here.

Pyniero   How – To what end?

Panura A good one:
To give ye knowledge of my new-born Mistress,
And in what doubt Armusia stands;

Pyniero   The damn'd Priest –

Panura   Sure he's a cruel man, methinks Religion
             Should teach more temperate lessons.

Pyniero   Wilt thou do one thing bravely?

Panura   Any good I am able.

Pyniero   Durst thou but guide me presently
             Through the same vault thou cam'st into the Palace,
             And those I shall appoint, such as I think fit?

Panura   Yes, I will do it, and suddenly, and truly.

Pyniero   I must needs steal that Priest, steal him, and hang him.

Panura   Do any thing to remove his mischief, strangle him –

Pyniero   Come prithee love.

Panura   You'll offer me no foul play?
             The Vault is dark.

Pyniero   'Twas well remember'd.

Panura   And ye may –
             But I hold ye honest.

Pyniero   Honest enough, I warrant thee.

Panura   I am but a poor weak wench.

Pyniero   If thou dost fear me,
             Why dost thou put me in mind?

Panura   To let you know sir,
             Though it be in your power,
             Yet a true gentleman –

Pyniero   I know what he'll do:
             Come and remember me, and I'll answer thee,

I'll answer thee to the full; we'll call at th'Castle,
And then my good guide do thy will; shalt find me
A very tractable man.

Panura   I hope I shall sir.

                                                    Exeunt

SCENE FIVE

Enter Bakam and Syana

Bakam   Let my men guard the gates.

Syana   And mine the Temple,
For fear the honour of our gods should suffer,
And on your lives be watchful.

Bakam   And be valiant;
And let's see, if these Portugals dare enter;
What their high hearts dare do: Let's see how readily,
The great Ruy Dias will redeem his Countryman;
He speaks proud words, and threatens.

Syana   He is approv'd sir,
And will put fair for what he promises;
I would wish friendlier terms, yet for our Liberties,
And for our gods, we are bound in our best service
Even in the hazard of our lives.

                        Enter the King above

King   Come up Princes,
And give your counsels, and your helps: the Fort still
Plays fearfully upon us, beats our buildings,
And turns our people wild with fears.

Bakam   Send for the prisoner,
And give us leave to argue.

                              [*Exeunt Bakam and Syana*]

*Enter Ruy Dias, Emanuel, Christophero,
Pedro, with Soldiers*

Ruy Dias   Come on nobly,
And let the Fort play still, we are strong enough
To look upon 'em, and return at pleasure;
It may be on our view they will return him.

Christophero   We will return 'em such thanks else, shall make 'em
Scratch where it itches not.

Emanuel   How the people stare,
And some cry, some pray, and some curse heartily: –
But it is the King –

Enter Syana, Bakam, Quisara, Armusia, with Soldiers above

Ruy Dias   I cannot blame their wisdoms,
They are all above; Armusia chain'd and bound too?
O these are thankful Squires.

Bakam   Hear us Ruy Dias,
Be wise and hear us, and give speedy answer:
Command thy Cannon presently to cease,
No more to trouble the afflicted People,
Or suddenly Armusia's head goes off,
As suddenly as said.

Emanuel   Stay Sir, be moderate.

Armusia   Do nothing that's dishonourable Ruy Dias,
Let not the fear of me master thy valour;
Pursue 'em still, they are base malicious people.

King   Friend be not desperate.

in undisgused

Armusia	I scorn your courtesies;
	Strike when you dare, a fair aim guide the Gunner,
	And let the palace burn first, then the Temples,
	And on their scorn'd gods erect my monument:
	Touch not the Princess, as you are a soldier.
Quisara	Which way you go, sir, I must follow necessary.
	One life, and one death.
King	Will you take a truce yet?

Enter Pyniero, Soza, and Soldiers
with the Governor disguised

Pyniero	No, no, go on: look here your god, your Prophet.
King	How came he taken?
Pyniero	I conjur'd for him, King.
	A terrier I; I earth'd him, and then snapp'd him.
Soza	Saving the reverence of your grace, we stole him
	E'en out of the next chamber to ye.
Pyniero	Come, come, begin King,
	Begin this bloody matter when you dare;
	And yet I scorn my sword should touch the rascal,
	I'll tear him thus before ye.

[*Pulls his Beard and hair off*]

Ha! What art thou?

King	How's this! Art thou a Prophet?
Ruy Dias	Come down Princes.
King	We are abus'd – Oh my most dear Armusia –
	Off with his chains. And now my noble sister,
	Rejoice with me, I know ye are pleas'd as I am

[*Exeunt those above*]

Recognition scene *King a Christian*

Pyniero	This is a precious Prophet. Why Don Governor, What make you here? How long have you taken orders?
Ruy Dias	Why what a wretch art thou to work this mischief! To assume this holy shape to ruin honour, Honour and chastity?

Enter King, and all from above

Governor	I had paid you all, But fortune play'd the slut. Come, give me my doom.
King	I cannot speak for wonder.
Governor	Nay, 'tis I sir, And here I stay your sentence.
King	Take her friend, You have half persuaded me to be a Christian, And with her all the joys, and all the blessings. Why what dream have we dwelt in?
Ruy Dias	All peace to ye, And all the happiness of heart swell with ye, Children as sweet and noble as their Parents.
Pyniero	And Kings at least.
Armusia	Good Sir forget my rashness. And noble Princes, for I was once angry, And out of that might utter some distemper, Think not 'tis my nature.
Syana	Your joy is ours sir, And nothing we find in ye, but most noble.
King	To prison with this dog, there let him howl, And if he can repent, sigh out his villainies: His Island we shall seize into our hands; The Castle where I lay most miserable,

Signior Pyniero I bestow on you;
The rest of next command upon these gentlemen,
Upon ye all, my love.

Armusia   O brave Ruy Dias,
You have started now beyond me. I must thank ye,
And thank ye for my life, my wife and honour.

Ruy Dias   I am glad I had her for you sir.

King   Come Princes,
Come friends and lovers all, come noble gentlemen,
No more guns now, nor hates, but joys and triumphs,
And universal gladness fly about us:
And know however subtle men dare cast,
And promise wrack, the gods give peace at last.

Exeunt

FINIS